Arts & Crafts for ⌂ *Home Decorating*®

'TIS THE SEASON

CREATIVE CHRISTMAS DECORATING

CREATIVE
PUBLISHING
international

Copyright © 1998 Creative Publishing international, Inc.

18705 Lake Drive East, Chanhassen, Minnesota 55317 • 1-800-328-3895 • www.creativepub.com • All rights reserved

Cataloging-in-Publication Data can be found on page 128

TABLE OF CONTENTS

'TIS THE SEASON

Christmas is a time to celebrate, sharing joys and gifts and time-honored traditions. It's also our favorite season for crafting and elaborate decorating.

Christmas decorations along your walkway and entry announce that your home is filled with holiday spirit. Twinkling lights brighten the nights; festive wreaths and natural arrangements send welcome messages by day.

Handcrafted treasures gladden every corner of our homes at Christmas. From the mantel to the tree, on furniture and walls, reminders of the season set a merry mood.

This is the season for entertaining. Seasonal celebrations with family and friends are enhanced with heartfelt greetings and personalized gifts.

Brighten dark winter nights and welcome evening guests with glowing spheres of miniature lights that will melt into your landscape during the day. Or build a tree of glistening lights to illuminate your walkway. Shape natural evergreens into a giant snowflake wreath, or transform a simple wreath into classic golden elegance with textured fruits, nuts, and cones. Or, if you prefer a rustic look, roll a birch-bark sconce for a wintery floral arrangement. Welcome birds to your yard with grain stands and suet feeders that offer edible embellishments and their favorite warming foods.

Bring a festive Christmas shine to your home by creating special decorations. Adorn your tree with a gilded tree topper, ornaments made of beads, ribbons, or seashells, and a merry patchwork Santa tree skirt. Complement your tree skirt with a matching wall quilt. Dress up your mantel with a shaped cloth, and hang a boot stocking at the fireplace to welcome Santa. Display soft snow figures, and set small trees all decked out in seashells throughout the house. Toss pillows made just for the season, or transform your current pillow collection with simple covers. Enjoy counting down to Christmas Day with an Advent wreath or calendar that shows off your favorite holiday mementos or cookies.

Share the joys of holiday celebrations with friends. Create a cascading centerpiece of glittering fruits and roses. Display it on a unique table runner that can be converted into placemats for two or more. Deliver kitchen treasures in bottles and jars decorated with items that enhance their special contents. Create keepsake gift wrapping by painting merry Santa boxes and bags. Or slip small mementos and favorite treats into toasty mittens trimmed with gossamer feathers or warm fur. Send one-of-kind paper art cards to greet friends far and near, or use miniature versions of the cards as gift tags, place cards, and special year-end thank-you notes.

Christmas decorations along your walkway and entry announce that your home is filled with holiday spirit. Twinkling lights brighten the nights; festive wreaths and natural arrangements send welcome messages by day.

SNOWFLAKE WREATH

Create this unique evergreen snowflake wreath, naturally embellished with pinecones, to greet holiday visitors. Select from a wide variety of natural pine branches for a needle style that appeals to you. Use short needles for a full wreath or long, feathery needles for a more open wreath. Also consider how needle density will affect the wreath's crystalline design.

Gather or purchase a few pinecones to cluster at the center. Choose cones matching in size and shape, or search for a variety of cones to add interest. Add holly or other greens with a contrasting color and texture to the center.

Spray green needles with an aerosol colorant, such as a white enamel paint or a flocking medium, or add a festive touch using an iridescent or glitter spray.

Wear work gloves to protect your hands from sharp needles.

MATERIALS

* Six natural pine spray branches, with or without pinecones; 18" (46 cm) long for 32" (81.5 cm) wreath.

* Green floral wire, 24-gauge; wire cutter; work gloves.

* Pinecones as desired; hot glue gun, optional.

* Fresh, dried, or artificial greens for center embellishment.

* Aerosol colorant, optional.

HOW TO MAKE
A SNOWFLAKE WREATH

1 Trim foliage from lower 7" (18 cm) of two branches; save trimmings. Lap bare lengths so branch tips are 32" (81.5 cm) apart; bind branches together at each end, using floral wire. Repeat twice to prepare three sets. Arrange sets so branches form small triangle at wreath center; bind branches at each intersection, using wire.

(Continued)

HOW TO MAKE A SNOWFLAKE WREATH
(CONTINUED)

2 Select six or more small branches for center; use trimmings from step 1. Arrange branches so they meet at center and just cover bare branches; point all needles away from center. Secure at triangle, using wire.

3 Wrap 9" (23 cm) wire around bottom layers of larger pinecones; twist to secure. Insert wires near wreath center; twist wires on back to secure. Trim excess wire. Layer small cones on larger, using hot glue. Embellish center of wreath with other greens.

4 Secure twisted wire loop at center back of upper branch, for hanging. Apply colorant to wreath, if desired; spray from top to cover upper and extended edges, or spray the entire wreath.

MORE IDEAS FOR SNOWFLAKE WREATHS

Purchase seven artificial sprays for a wreath that will last many years; cut seventh spray for small branches. Bend wire core to secure at center. Arrange clustered cones in a star formation.

Add battery-operated lights; secure hidden battery pack on back. Replace pinecones with elements that reflect other holiday decorations, such as shell ornaments (page 44), silver bells, or other dried pods; avoid using embellishments that may be damaged by nature.

CLASSICAL GOLD WREATH

Transform an artificial evergreen wreath into an elegant display of classic golden nature with textured fruits, gilded nuts, and dried artichokes.

Give inexpensive artificial fruits a rich, dramatic surface, using a texturizing medium such as DecoArt™ Decorating Paste™. Then paint them with an antique crackled finish, touched with gold.

HOW TO MAKE A CLASSICAL GOLD WREATH

MATERIALS

* Artificial evergreen wreath.
* Artificial fruit stems.
* Texturizing medium; craft stick.
* Crackle medium; small sponge applicator.
* Off-white acrylic craft paint.
* Antiquing medium and soft cloth.
* Gold wax-base paint.
* Dried artichokes; gold aerosol paint.
* Pinecones; glossy aerosol wood tone, optional.
* Assorted nuts; hot glue gun.
* Green floral wire, 24-gauge; wire cutter.
* Dried floral material.

1 Apply rough coat of texturizing paste to fruits, using craft stick. Dollop and spread paste in some areas; leave some areas bare. Allow to dry thoroughly. Brush crackle medium on fruits; allow to set.

2 Brush off-white paint on fruit, leaving some original fruit color showing; paint will crackle almost immediately. Allow to dry. Apply stain, using cloth; wipe off excess.

(Continued)

3 Lightly rub gold paint on areas of fruits and nuts. Paint artichokes gold. Spray pinecones with glossy wood tone, if desired.

4 Secure fruit stem ends at center top of wreath; wrap wreath branches around stems. Weave fruit stems partially around wreath, leaving bottom of wreath bare; secure with wreath branches.

5 Wrap wires around bottom layers of pinecones; twist to secure, leaving long tails. Insert wires at center top of wreath so pinecones hang into opening; twist wires at back.

6 Wrap wires around artichokes, as in step 5; secure in arc over pinecones. Secure dried floral stems, evenly spaced, around wreath, using wreath branches. Secure nuts, using hot glue.

MORE IDEAS FOR CLASSICAL GOLD ARRANGEMENTS

Plant a small tree in a classic urn; weave a decorative ribbon and small lights through its branches, and embellish it with assorted textured fruits and golden artichokes. Arrange larger fruits at the bottom and smaller fruits near the top.

Hang a garland so it cascades down the sides of the door or across balcony and porch railings. Scatter fruits, artichokes, nuts, and ferns throughout its length. Weave ribbon in and out of garland.

BIRCH-BARK SCONCE

Hung on the door or beneath a porch light, this birch-bark sconce arrangement is a rustic celebration of the season.

Dramatic color variations occur naturally in birch bark; the papery white surface peels to reveal a peach core, and dark, rough blemishes are common. Lichen and mushrooms grow in wonderful clusters, adding more

colors and textures. Birch bark may be gathered from fallen trees or purchased at floral shops.

The tefe rose is an exploded seed pod attached to stem wire; it resembles a blossoming flower and is available at floral shops.

Assorted evergreens, such as fir, spruce, cedar, boxwood, and juniper, are appropriately used alone or mixed.

HOW TO MAKE A BIRCH-BARK SCONCE ARRANGEMENT

MATERIALS

* Birch-bark piece, at least 14" × 6" (35.5 × 15 cm); six to eight screws, depending on bark size; utility knife, optional.
* Leather lacing, length depending on bark size; leather needle; clip.
* Floral foam; serrated knife.
* Three tefe roses.
* Assorted evergreen sprigs; seeded eucalyptus.
* Floral stem wire; floral tape; wire cutters.
* Bell reed stems.
* Three brass jingle bells.

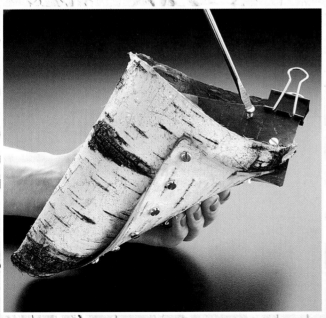

1 Tear or cut birch bark to desired size. Soak bark in very hot water until pliable, at least one hour. Roll cone, taking advantage of unique characteristics of bark; leave opening at bottom and clamp upper edge with clip. Twist screws through lapped ends to make four to six holes. Twist two screws through bark, near top of back.

2 Cut 9" (23 cm) from lacing; secure at back, for hanger. Knot end of remaining lacing; insert other end at inside bottom of cone, using leather needle, if desired. Weave lacing through holes; remove screws as needed. Knot lacing on inside; turn lacing over upper edge, to outside. Cut foam to fit sconce, using serrated knife; place in sconce.

(Continued)

3 Insert longest rose at back; insert other roses at front sides. Bend front roses slightly forward. Insert evergreens and eucalyptus, distributing variations throughout arrangement; lengthen stems, using wire and floral tape, if necessary.

4 Cut assorted lengths from bell reed stems; scatter reeds throughout arrangement. Attach jingle bells and evergreen sprigs to lacing tail as desired.

— MORE IDEAS FOR SCONCE FILLERS —

Depict a Christmas carol by using holly and ivy stems. Secure the sconce using narrow ribbon or cord; replace the bells with a bow.

Repeat the natural colors of the bark, using giant lotus pods, green or brown eucalyptus, and sage or salal. Dangle pinecones.

LIGHT SPHERE

This glorious sphere of small lights will brighten your outdoor decorating in a unique way. It blends into the natural setting of your yard during the day and explodes into color or bright white at night.

Purchase a package of clear plastic party glasses and simply melt them together to create the sphere. Choose multicolored lights or a string of single-color or white lights. Suspend the spheres from tree branches, and enjoy!

HOW TO MAKE A LIGHT SPHERE

MATERIALS

* Fifty clear, flexible plastic old-fashioned glasses with slanted sides.
* Hot glue gun.

* Weatherproof string of 50 or 100 miniature lights.
* Weather-resistant cord, for hanger.
* Outdoor-rated extension cord; brown duct tape.

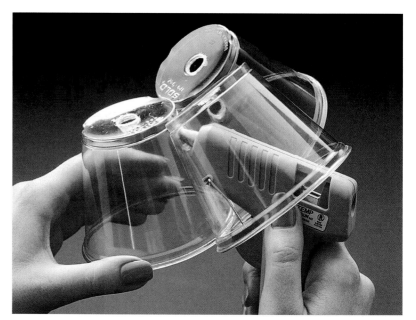

1 Make hole in bottom of each glass, using hot glue gun tip; rotate gun to make hole large enough to fit one or two lights.

2 Hold two glasses together so top and bottom edges meet. Fuse glasses together as near bottom as possible; press glue gun tip to inside of one glass until hole begins to form, then quickly press tip at same point in other glass, melting glasses together. Allow plastic to cool. Fuse third glass to both of joined glasses. Test joints for stability.

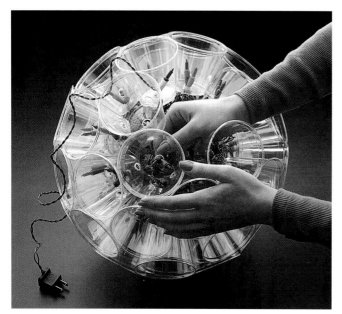

3 Continue adding glasses, fusing adjacent glasses, to form sphere; leave opening to fit hand. Place light string inside sphere; allow plug and cord to hang outside. Insert one or two lights into bottom hole of each glass, using all lights.

4 Thread cord through fusing holes in opening row; pull up three evenly spaced loops, and knot together. Suspend sphere as desired.

5 Secure plug end of extension cord to tree trunk, using duct tape; position cord so light strand will reach it without stretching. Plug cord into outdoor-rated circuit receptacle. Plug lights into outlet; wrap light strand around nearby twig or branch to prevent unneccessary stress on lights.

— MORE IDEAS FOR LIGHT SPHERES —

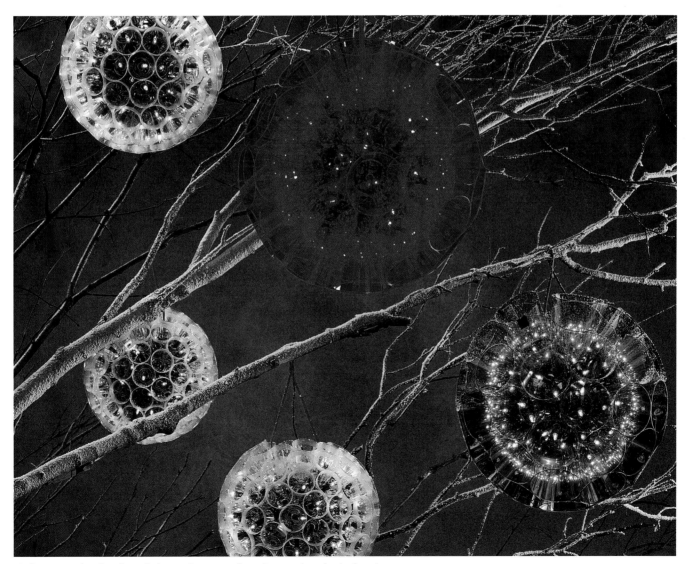

Substitute colored or faceted glasses. Create smaller spheres, using plastic shot glasses.

TOPIARY OF LIGHTS

Create this small, shaped tree of miniature lights for a delightful way to mark your entry and to brighten steps during dark winter nights.

Wrap a tomato cage with garland and small lights; use two light strings to maximize points of light within safety regulations. Place it on top of an empty urn for a classic topiary, or on a large overturned terra-cotta saucer for a tiny country tree.

HOW TO MAKE A TOPIARY OF LIGHTS

MATERIALS

- Tomato cage, 30" (76 cm) high.
- Galvanized steel wire, 12-gauge; wire cutter.
- Electrical tape.

- 16 yd. (14.72 m) metallic garland.
- Two weatherproof, end-to-end strings of 100 miniature lights.
- Outdoor-rated extension cord.

1 Turn cage upside down. Cut three wire pieces 1" (2.5 cm) longer than existing supports. Bend back 1" (2.5 cm) around bottom hoop. Secure wires to hoops halfway between supports, using electrical wire. Tape all wires together at top. Secure one light string at top; drop male plug so it rests easily on ground.

2 Secure end of garland to top of cage. Wrap garland around cage toward bottom, holding lights out of way. Join garland lengths as necessary to cover cage. Wrap light string around cage; turn bulbs out as string winds toward bottom. Join light strings as necessary, hiding plug ends in garland. Plug lights into cord; plug cord into outdoor-rated circuit receptacle. Fluff garland to partially cover strings. Place tree on urn or at side of steps.

BIRD FEEDERS

Sharing the joy of the season with feathered friends is a tradition in many parts of the world, especially where winter snows make food hard to find.

Birds gather at grain sources; they like regular and bearded wheat, oats, barley, millet, sorghum, and foxtail. Miniature corn and dried sunflowers are other favorites, and many birds love raw peanuts. Seeds may be pressed into a layer of peanut butter spread over cones. Breads and popcorn should be avoided; they are filling and don't provide sufficient energy. Suet is a favorite attraction because it provides long-lasting, warming energy. Plain suet is available at groceries; garden centers and specialty bird-feed stores offer suet blended with nuts and grains.

Assorted berries, such as cranberries, holly, bittersweet, rose hips, and red pepperberries, provide colorful embellishments as well as food; avoid using dyed naturals or imitations. Small fresh fruits, such as crabapples and kumquats, are sweet treats. Dried fruit slices may be purchased or dried at home in a dehydrator or oven. Use well-colored, unblemished fruits, such as apples, oranges, and pomegranates; choose firm citrus with thick rinds and minimal juice. Small cones, colorful peppers, and a variety of pods, such as lotus and poppy, may be added for interest.

Bird feeders also attract squirrels, which easily jump to feeders from overhanging branches or roofs. Metal hardware cloth discourages their visits to suet feeders; a convenient bowl of shelled corn will delight them.

HOW TO OVEN-DRY FRESH FRUIT FOR EMBELLISHMENTS

Soak apple slices in 1 qt. (0.9 L) water with 2 tbsp. (25 mL) lemon juice, to prevent discoloration. Pat dry, using paper towel. Arrange ¼" (6 mm) slices of assorted fruits on baking sheet; separate slightly. Place in slow oven set at 200°F (95°C); use exhaust fan to remove humidity as fruit dries. Bake about two hours; timing varies with fleshiness and quantity of fruit. Remove when fruit is leathery.

HOW TO BUILD A SUET HOUSE

MATERIALS

* ⅔ yd. (0.63 m) rough-sawn 1 × 8 cedar or redwood; saw.
* Drill; drill bits in assorted sizes.
* Four galvanized screws, 1½" (3.8 cm) long.
* ½" (1.3 cm) hardware cloth, cut into two 6" × 4½" (15 × 11.5 cm) pieces; staple gun.
* 1 yd. (0.95 m) heavy leather lacing or polyurethane cord; two screw eyes.
* Embellishments as desired; string or raffia.
* Suet block, about 4½" × 4½" × 1½" (11.5 × 11.5 × 3.8 cm).

CUTTING DIRECTIONS

Cut one 8" (20.5 cm) length of wood, for the base. Cut one 8" × 5" (20.5 × 12.5 cm) piece, for the roof. Cut two 1¾" × 5" (4.5 × 12.5 cm) pieces, for the uprights. Include knots, if desired; avoid placing any knots near the center of the short sides on the base and roof, and near the ends of the uprights.

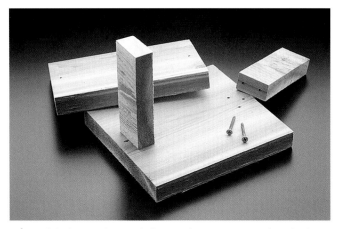

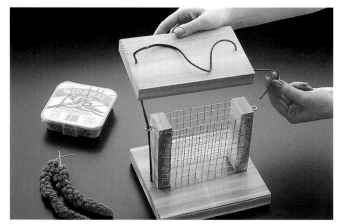

1 Drill hole ½" (1.3 cm) from edge, at center of each short side of base, using drill bit in same diameter as lacing. Repeat on roof. Drill two ⅛" (3 mm) holes on each short side of base, drilling each hole ½" (1.3 cm) from center and 1⅛" (2.8 cm) from edge. Drill two ⅛" (3 mm) holes on center line of one upright end, 1" (2.5 cm) apart; repeat on other upright. Secure uprights to base, inserting screws through small holes from underside of base.

2 Secure hardware cloth to upright sides, using staples. Drill hole on outside of each upright, ⅜" (1 cm) from top; insert screw eyes. Knot lacing end. Slip lacing from base bottom through screw eye, roof holes, opposite screw eye, and return to base bottom; knot loose end. Tie knot near lacing center to form 3" (7.5 cm) loop, for hanger. Insert suet into holder; tie other edibles to screw eyes, using string or raffia.

HOW TO MAKE A GRAIN STAND

MATERIALS

* Container, such as wooden tote, window box, terra-cotta pot, or urn.
* Sand to fill container; paper.
* Grain stalks; string.
* Birdseed as desired.
* Embellishments as desired.

1 Measure container depth. Trim grain stalks so total length is no more than five times container depth; tie bundles near the center, using string.

2 Line container with paper to prevent sand spills; partially fill container with sand. Push bundles to container bottom; add additional sand, and top with birdseed to container rim. Embellish container with greens, berries, or grain garlands as desired.

Purchase bell-shaped suet or seed; *secure embellishments to edible hanger.*

Fill pomegranate or citrus shell *with suet or seed. Cut fruit in half; scoop sections and seeds out. Punch three evenly spaced holes around shell, ⅜" (1 cm) from rim. Slip cord through each hole and knot ends, to hang; allow shell to air-dry several days before filling. Secure edible embellishments to cord, if desired.*

Fill a birch-bark sconce *with wheat stalks. Secure the stalks, using a suet plug, and add orange slices for colorful nourishment. Insert evergreen sprigs along the upper edge, for perch.*

Handcrafted treasures gladden every corner of our homes at Christmas. From the mantel to the tree, on furniture and walls, reminders of the season set a merry mood.

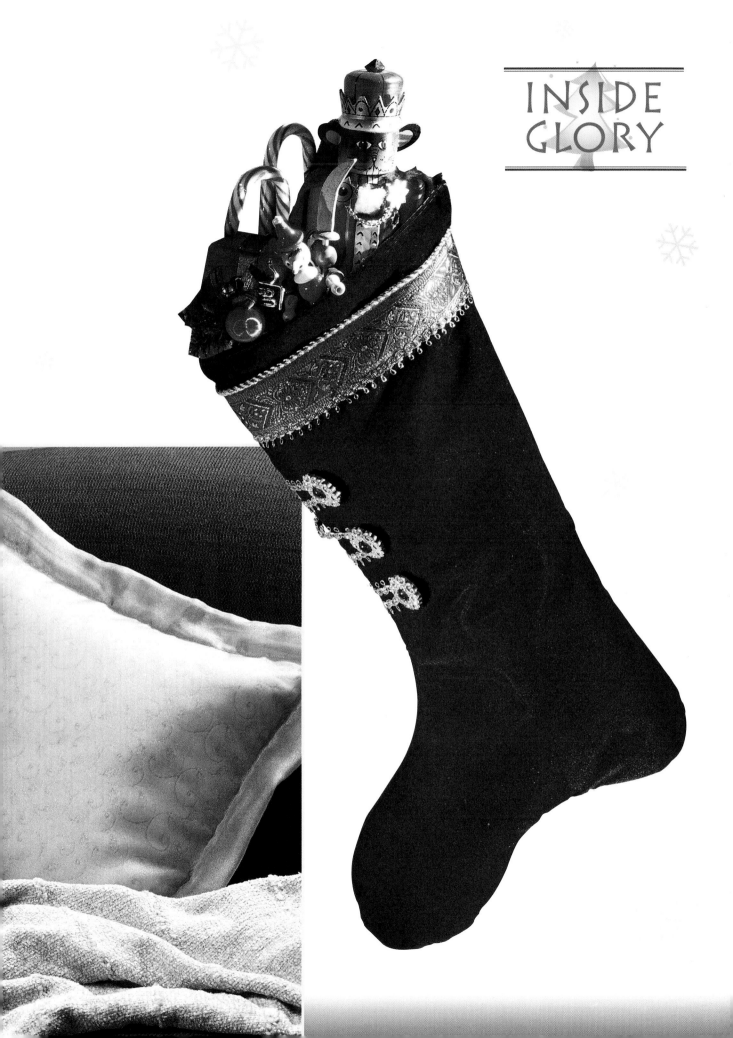

STAR TREE TOPPER

Create this lightweight, beautiful star for a glorious tree topper. Form a raised design on a papier mâché star using hot glue. Apply spray paint, small sheets of imitation metal leaf, and an antiquing medium to give it a special glow.

Purchase a papier mâché star; several styles are available in craft stores, including tree-topper cones. Play with various letters of the alphabet to make a design that complements your star; simply connect elongated S and C curves for intricate scroll designs, and join mirror images of the connected letters with a V to fill a star's point.

Paint the star before applying metal leaf for an interesting secondary color; the leaf will split slightly and reveal the color around the raised design. Select gold, silver, or copper leaf to complement your other ornaments. Age bright metallic finishes with an antiquing medium, if desired.

Secure the star to your tree-top using elastic cord. Use decorative gold or silver cords to match the star's finish, or choose white or black cords so they will disappear among flocked or natural needles.

MATERIALS

* Papier mâché star in desired style.

* Hot glue gun.

* Acrylic paint, dark red, black, or green.

* Metal-leaf adhesive; brush.

* Imitation metal leaf in desired color; soft brush, optional.

* Antiquing medium in desired color; soft brush; soft cloth.

* Aerosol clear acrylic sealer.

* 1/3 yd. (0.32 m) elastic cord; curved upholstery needle, optional.

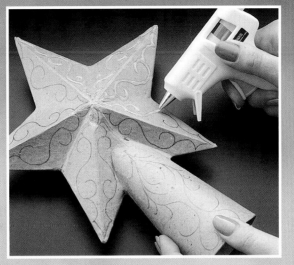

1 Draw lines for raised design on star, using pencil. Apply hot glue to design lines, holding glue gun at 45° angle while gently squeezing. Keep tip slightly above star surface until line ends; touch tip to line end, and lift straight up. Allow to harden and cool. Repeat on back, if desired.

2 Paint star, using acrylic paint. Allow to dry. Apply leaf adhesive to star; allow to set, following manufacturer's directions.

3 Cut metal leaf into manageable pieces. Apply metal leaf to surface, following manufacturer's directions. Apply clear acrylic sealer; allow to dry.

4 Apply antiquing medium, following manufacturer's directions, if desired. Wipe off excess, using soft cloth; allow some to remain in crevices around design. Apply clear acrylic sealer; allow to dry.

For stars without tree-topper cone, cut elastic cord in half. Insert one end through curved upholstery needle; push needle through star back so it pierces star each side of center. Pull cord half-way through star; knot ends loosely. Pull second cord through star back, 2" to 3" (5 to 7.5 cm) below first one; knot ends. Slip cords over vertical branch at treetop. Adjust knots to tighten loops, if necessary; rotate knots to star surface.

Beaded fruit in a bowl (above) offers holiday sparkle for the buffet or coffee table.

Three-dimensional pearl cage (left) showcases a glimmering trinket.

Shimmering crystal bead icicles (opposite) drip from the tree.

BEADED ORNAMENTS

Create a beautiful collection of beaded ornaments for your tree and home. Add elegant crystal icicles to your tree, or hang them in a window for rainbows of light. Hang three-dimensional cages to enjoy their pattern of beads; use them to emphasize a special ornament or suspend a sprig of mistletoe. Colorful fruits and balls make trees special; gather them in a bowl for unique centerpieces.

Select beads in a variety of colors, shapes, and sizes for added interest. Consider crystal and pearl beads for an elegant look, or use wooden beads for a casual country home; use metallic beads with any style.

Purchase unique beads individually or buy bulk packages to arrange a variety of bead patterns. Beads of uniform size and color also come in prestrung hanks of 10 or 12 strings; although many colors are available, you may choose to string your own beads for the fruit and ball ornaments.

HOW TO MAKE AN ICICLE

MATERIALS

* Crystal or metallic beads in assorted sizes and colors.
* 24-gauge wire; wire cutter; needlenose pliers.

1 Arrange beads in a line according to size, alternating colors and shapes as desired. Measure approximate length; cut wire about 2" (5 cm) longer.

2 Form small loop in wire end, using pliers. Slide smallest bead onto other end; continue, working from smallest to largest bead, stacking beads snug. Trim excess wire ¾" (2 cm) from largest bead; form wire loop for attaching hanger.

HOW TO MAKE A THREE-DIMENSIONAL CAGE

MATERIALS

* 24-gauge wire; wire cutter; permanent marker; pliers.
* Beads in desired sizes.

* Small decorative ornament, if desired.
* ½ yd. (0.5 m) ribbon, ⅛" (3 mm) wide, for bow.

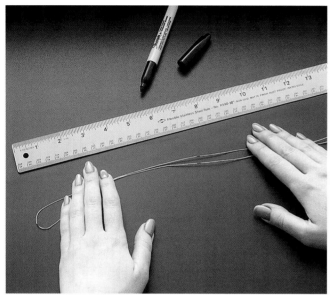

1 Form wire loop to determine desired ornament size; consider size of suspended ornament, if one will be used. Cut wire with length equal to three times the determined measurement plus 3" (7.5 cm). Mark wire center, using marker. Measure half the original wire loop length to each side of center; mark.

2 Slide beads onto wire, forming symmetrical arrangement on each side of center. Snug beads to fill space between outer marks; twist wire at marks, forming loop. Mark the original wire loop length to each side of twist; mark halfway points.

3 Slide beads onto wire to fill space from twist to first mark; follow original arrangement, if desired. Wrap wire at mark between beads at wire's center. Slide beads onto wire to fill space to next mark, using same arrangement, if desired; wrap wire around first twist to complete circle.

4 Repeat step 3 with remaining wire. Suspend inner ornament, if desired, using fine cord or wire; secure at top twist. Use one wire to form loop for attaching hanger; trim excess wire. Attach ribbon or cord to loop for hanging.

HOW TO MAKE BEADED FRUITS & BALLS

MATERIALS

* Styrofoam® or lightweight wood forms as desired; use six balls for grape cluster.

* Ribbon or cord, for hanging.

* Toothpicks; craft glue.

* Drill and small drill bit, optional.

* Prestrung seed or rochaille beads; 3½" (9 cm) forms and clusters of six 1" (2.5 cm) grapes use about one hank of 12 strings. Or bulk beads; beading needle; thread.

* Embellishments as desired; green floral wire and silk ivy leaves, for grape cluster.

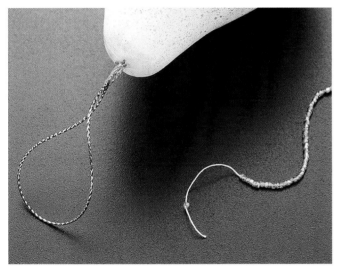

1 Create small hole at form top, using toothpick or small drill bit. Cut desired ribbon or cord length for hanger. Apply small amount of glue to ends; insert ends into hole, forming hanger. Allow to dry. Separate bead hank strings; tie knot to secure end beads.

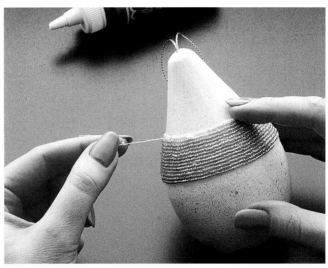

2 Apply small glue band at form center; allow glue to set two or three minutes until tacky. Wrap bead string over glue, spiraling upward around form; apply more glue, and place strings end to end as necessary to cover upper half. Repeat to cover lower half. Allow to dry; trim excess bead strings. Embellish as desired.

For striped balls, alternate bead colors; start and finish each string at back of ball.

For grape cluster, wrap green floral wire around nail for tendril; twist around hanger base or glue to form as desired. Create five more grapes; cluster so each grape touches three or four others; glue. Add silk leaves as desired.

VICTORIAN ORNAMENTS

Visit the romance of the Victorian era with these two ornaments. Cover Styrofoam® forms with delicate netting or narrow ribbon. Adorn them with metal or resin Victorian charms, beads, and decorative trims, such as cording, ribbon, and gimp. Secure embellishments with craft glue or with escutcheon or dressmaker pins, for quick and easy finishing.

HOW TO MAKE A VICTORIAN CHARM ORNAMENT

MATERIALS

* Styrofoam form, 3½" to 4" (9 to 10 cm) tall.
* Acrylic paint, in desired colors.
* ¾ yd. (0.7 m) cording, lace, or ribbon.
* ½ yd. (0.5 m) tulle or sparkle illusion.
* Victorian charms as desired; hot glue gun.
* Beads and sequins as desired; straight or escutcheon pins.

1 Paint form as desired; allow to dry. Tie small knots at trim ends to prevent raveling, if necessary. Tie square knot to form 3" (7.5 cm) loop at trim center. Set form on 15" (38 cm) tulle square. Gather tulle firmly at top. Place trim knot at back; tie bow in front to secure tulle.

2 Paint resin charms, if desired. Apply charms to front and back as desired, using hot glue. Apply beads as desired, using brass pins.

HOW TO MAKE A RIBBON BALL ORNAMENT

MATERIALS

* 10 yd. (9.15 m) ribbon, ¼" to ⅜" (6 mm to 1 cm) wide.
* 3" (7.5 cm) Styrofoam ball.
* Craft glue.
* Two or more beads as desired.
* Straight or escutcheon pins as desired.
* Embellishments as desired.

1 Secure end of ribbon to ball, using glue. Wrap ribbon very taut around ball, overlapping ribbon slightly, until ball is covered. Pull end of ribbon tight; secure at top of ball, using glue. Hold firmly until dry.

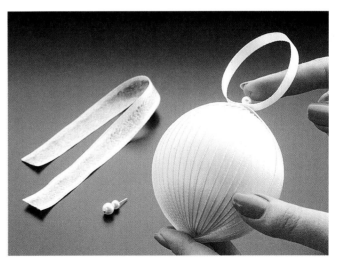

2 Leave 6" (15 cm) ribbon tail, for loop; glue end to top, forming loop. Pin bead, using straight or escutcheon pin, at top and bottom to prevent ribbon layers from slipping. Secure additional trims or beads as desired.

SHELL ORNAMENTS

Many areas of the world do not experience drifts of holiday snow; some people prefer warm days on the beach. These lovely ornaments are made of assorted seashells; they bring some of nature's beauty indoors, and they unite traditions of warm and cold climates.

Conical shells may be professionally cut; slices reveal the delicate patterns of the body cavity, and lily cuts resemble the furled petals of a flower. Umbonium shells are naturally compressed, with a buttonlike look.

Natural variations in bivalve shells can be used in the design of angel ornaments; some shells have "shoulders" at the hinge. Surface textures and color patterns may suggest gown folds, ruffles, and more.

Purchase sliced and lily-cut shells at nature shops or coastal tourist shops. Buy whole shells and miniature embellishments, or gather interesting pieces at the beach for added memories.

Consider how shells will relate in size and shape to others chosen for the same ornament; play with various pieces until they are pleasing to the eye. Look for a shallow halo shell if the body shell is deep; select a deep halo to cup the head if the body is nearly flat.

Use small sea life to embellish the angel. Choose a simple sea star heart, a broken shard trumpet, or tiny barnacle eyes. Discover tiny doves inside a sand dollar to imitate rays of halo light.

HOW TO MAKE A SEASHELL SNOWFLAKE ORNAMENT

MATERIALS

* 5" (12.5 cm) ribbon, ¼" (6 mm) wide, in desired color.
* 1" (2.5 cm) diameter plastic, wood, or tagboard disc.
* Six center-cut slices of equal length from chula or strawberry strombus seashells, for outer layer.
* Six lily-cut shells of equal length from chula or strawberry strombus seashells, for inner layer.
* One umbonium or snail shell, ¼" to ½" (6 mm to 1.3 cm) diameter, for center.
* Craft glue.

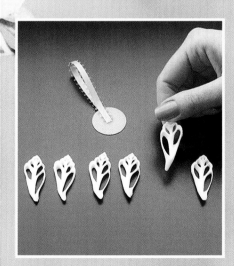

1 Lap ribbon ends to form loop; glue to disc, and allow to dry. Arrange chula slices side by side. Note curves and spaces; turn slices over as necessary so all longest spaces are on the same side.

2 Place ⅛" (3 mm) glue dot on underside of chula slice, at narrow tip. Lap about ½" (1.3 cm) of slice onto disc. Repeat quickly with remaining slices. Adjust lap amount so slices are evenly spaced on an imaginary circle. Allow to dry several hours.

3 Place ⅛" (3 mm) glue dot on lily-cut shell back, ¼" (6 mm) from narrow tip. Place tip over disc center so shell back rests between two slices and curled lip is on the top. Repeat quickly with remaining lily-cut shells; adjust so cut tops are evenly spaced on an imaginary circle. Glue umbonium shell at center to hide tips. Allow to dry overnight.

HOW TO MAKE A SEASHELL ANGEL ORNAMENT

MATERIALS

* ⅜" to ⅝" (1 to 1.5 cm) wood bead, for head; acrylic paints and fine-tip brush.
* 10" (25.5 cm) 8-lb. (3.5 kg) monofilament fishing line, for hanger.

* Craft glue; mat knife.
* Miniature shells, for hair.
* Round seashell, larger than head, for halo.
* Large attractive shell, for gown.

* Ribbon, felt, suede, or Ultrasuede® strip, ¼" to ½" (6 mm to 1.3 cm) wide, for wings; scissors.
* Embellishments as desired.

1 Paint eyes and mouth on head. Knot ends of hanger to form loop; secure to bead hole or back of head, using glue. Glue miniature shells to top and sides of head, for hair, bringing hair close to face to prevent appearance of baldness; leave back of head bare.

2 Apply glue to halo hinge. Place gown hinge over halo, lapping shells about ⅛" (3 mm). Secure head to halo bowl and snug against body, using glue. Allow to dry thoroughly; check shells occasionally to make sure they remain snug.

4 Apply glue along upper edge and hinge of gown; secure wings. Trim ends diagonally, pointing away from gown. Embellish as desired. Trim any visible glue from ornament with mat knife.

3 Cut wing strip equal in length to four times body height. Place glue drop at strip center; turn strip onto glue at slight diagonal to form loop that is slightly more than half the body width. Repeat to form second loop.

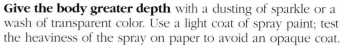

Substitute a small round seashell or piece of coral for the head; use small glass beads or loops of plain cotton string for hair.

Give the body greater depth with a dusting of sparkle or a wash of transparent color. Use a light coat of spray paint; test the heaviness of the spray on paper to avoid an opaque coat.

Collect broken or sand-washed shells, and consider design possibilities of the found treasures. Holes in small shells may be located perfectly for eyes or mouth; conical shells work well for the gown. Protruding nodules may imitate feet beneath a gown.

Use various shells for wings. Select pieces similar in size, shape, and color; they do not need to match. Arrange the wings behind the assembled angel, noting the contact points. Secure quickly, using hot glue; reinforce the bond, using craft glue.

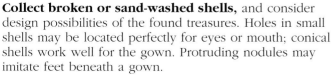

PATCHWORK SANTA TREE SKIRT

Five jolly Santa faces are the focus of this three-dimensional tree skirt. A button mouth and painted eyes show his delight, wire spectacles rest on his big round nose, and a jingle bell dangles from the tip of his hat. Quotable panels join the faces in traditional holiday colors.

Select white faux fur for Santa's beard and hat trim. Choose from small cotton prints or solid reds for suitable hat and lettering fabrics; select a contrasting green fabric for the rest of the skirt and skirt lining.

Use a rotary cutter and cutting surface, and a wide see-through straightedge with 45° angle markings for fast and easy cutting of the various pieces. Or develop paper patterns, using the measurements given in the cutting directions. Fold or stack most fabrics to speed cutting; cut faux fur one layer at a time to ensure accuracy.

All seam allowances are ¼" (6 mm). To maximize the beauty of the faux fur, turn its pile away from the cut edges when stitching and press seams lightly to avoid crushing the pile.

Use a nail polish or acrylic paint bottle, or some other small sturdy cylinder with a similar diameter, to shape Santa's glasses.

MATERIALS

* ¼ yd. (0.25 m) fabric, for face and nose.

* ½ yd. (0.5 m) white faux fur, for beard and hat trim.

* ⅜ yd. (0.35 m) red fabric, for hat, border, and letters.

* 1¾ yd. (1.6 m) green fabric, for skirt panel.

* 2 yd. (1.85 m) fabric, for skirt lining.

* Rotary cutter, cutting surface, straightedge, optional.

* Tracing paper.

* Blush; black fabric paint or permanent fabric marker or embroidery floss.

* Polyester fiberfill.

* Five ⅝" (1.5 cm) red buttons, for mouths.

* Five brass jingle bells, ½" to ⅝" (1.3 to 1.5 cm).

* 60" (152.5 cm) 24-gauge brass wire, for glasses; small cylinder; invisible thread.

* Paper-backed fusible web; iron.

* Polyester quilt batting, 1½ yd. (1.4 m) square.

CUTTING DIRECTIONS

Cut two 1½" (3.8 cm) strips from the face fabric, using a straightedge and a rotary cutter; stack the strips. Cut five quadrilaterals for the faces, as shown below, with sides that measure 12½" (31.8 cm) and 9½" (24.3 cm).

Draw a 3" (7.5 cm) diameter circle on paper; use it as a pattern to cut five noses.

Cut 2" (5 cm) faux fur strips into five quadrilaterals, as shown below, with sides that measure 10½" (26.8 cm) and 6½" (16.3 cm); repeat four times to cut five hat trim pieces.

Cut three 9" (23 cm) squares from faux fur; cut them in half diagonally for the beards. Discard one beard. Or, if fur has a nap, make a pattern first. Cut five beards with nap running toward point.

Cut three 5½" (14 cm) squares from the red fabric; stack the squares. Cut them in half diagonally for six hats; discard one hat.

Cut five 4" (10 cm) strips from green fabric; stack three strips. Cut quadrilaterals, as shown below, with sides that measure 16" (40.5 cm) and 8¼" (21.2 cm). Cut a total of ten border pieces.

Trace the pattern on page 119 for the hat tip, and cut five from the red fabric.

Enlarge the skirt panel pattern (page 125). Cut five panels; cut one panel in half from the tip to the mark.

Cut an 18" (46 cm) length of fabric across one end of the skirt lining.

HOW TO CUT QUADRILATERAL PIECES

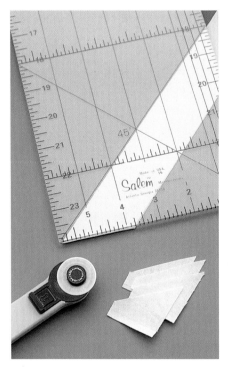

1 Align 45° angle mark of straightedge along one side of stacked strips; trim end of strips, holding straightedge firmly.

2 Mark long outer side and short inner side as required in cutting directions, using pencil; for example, measure 12½" (31.8 cm) from pointed end and 9½" (24.3 cm) from inner end, for face strips.

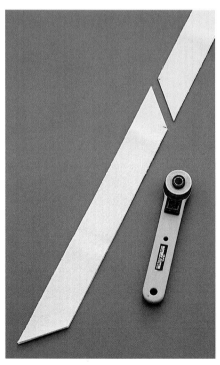

3 Reposition straightedge on marks; 45° angle mark will align with side of strip. Cut.

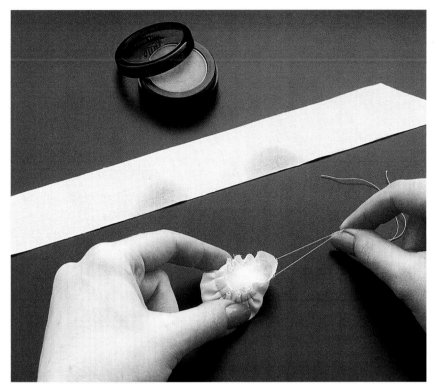

1 Apply two half circles of blush lightly to lower edge of face, for cheeks. Apply 1" (2.5 cm) circle of blush to center of nose circle. Machine-baste ¼" (6 mm) from cut edge of nose circle. Pull thread tails on right side of fabric tight, enclosing ball of fiberfill; knot, and trim tails.

2 Stitch long side of hat to short side of hat trim, right sides together. Stitch long sides of face and beard, right sides together. Stitch remaining sides of hat trim and face, right sides together. Press seams lightly toward hat and face.

3 Hand-stitch nose to center of face. Sew button on beard, for mouth; position directly beneath nose, about 1" (2.5 cm) from face seam.

(Continued)

4 Fold hat tip, right sides together, as indicated on pattern. Stitch from point B to point C; backstitch to secure each end. Turn right side out, aligning raw edges; press. Stitch jingle bell to point.

5 Pin hat tip to right side of hat, aligning raw edges along upper right side of hat, as shown.

6 Cut 12" (30.5 cm) length of wire. Lap ends, leaving 3/4" (2 cm) tails; wrap tails around wire to form circle.

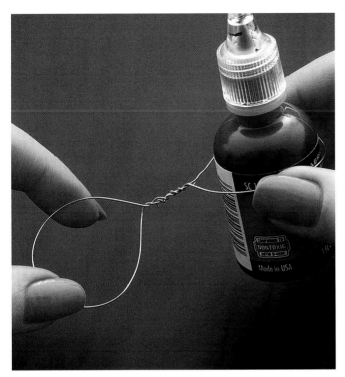

7 Twist circle once to form figure eight; position wrapped tails at center. Place one loop around cylinder, and twist center until loop is tight; remove cylinder. Repeat for opposite loop.

8 Bend twisted part slightly to form spectacles' bridge. Secure to face with a few stitches across bridge, using invisible thread. Draw eyes on face, using fabric paint or marker, or hand-stitch eyes, using floss.

HOW TO MAKE A SANTA TREE SKIRT

1 Make five Santa blocks, as on pages 51 and 52, steps 1 to 5. Mark wrong side of Santa blocks, panels, and borders where ¼" (6 mm) seams will intersect; place one mark at each corner.

2 Enlarge HO! pattern (page 125); trace on paper side of fusible web four times. Apply web to red fabric scraps, following manufacturer's directions; cut letters out and remove paper backing. Fuse one letter set on one skirt panel, as shown, following manufacturer's directions; repeat with three remaining sets and three whole panels.

(Continued)

3 Arrange blocks and panels as shown. Stitch adjoining block and panel sides, right sides together, backstitching at corner marks; keep jingle bell tip free.

4 Stitch adjoining short panel sides, backstitching ¼" (6 mm) from each end, as in step 3; leave long sides of two half panels open. Press the seam allowances toward panels.

5 Align short side of border piece to Santa beard; stitch as in step 3. Repeat with nine remaining border pieces. Stitch border end seams from corners to cut edges; press seam allowances toward borders.

6 Mark selvage center of larger lining piece; mark cut edge center of smaller lining piece. Align pieces, right sides together, matching marks. Stitch; press seam allowance to one side.

7 Place batting on work surface so it is smooth, but not stretched. Place lining over batting, right side up, and pieced top over lining, right side down. Pin layers together along all raw edges. Trim excess batting and lining, using pieced top as pattern.

8 Stitch around tree skirt; pivot at each seam, and leave 6" (15 cm) opening on one long panel side. Trim seam allowances at all outer corners; clip to stitching at all inner corners. Turn skirt right side out; press seams lightly.

9 Stitch in the ditch around blocks, and between all border and panel pieces. Stitch close to edges of all fused letters. Complete Santa block as on pages 52 and 53, steps 6 to 8. Slipstitch opening closed.

BOOT STOCKINGS

These fun stockings reflect two of the most recognized holiday traditions, Santa and the Nutcracker. Santa's boot is buckled and strapped and has feather trim lapping his pants leg. The Nutcracker's boot is decorated with festive trims and buttoned laces.

Create stockings to mirror your holiday decor. Choose velveteens, bejeweled buckles and buttons, and rayon or metallic frogs, for rich elegance. Select denims, corduroys, or wool flannels, with buckles left uncovered, for a laid-back Santa. Use similar fabrics with plain wood or metal buttons, for an American Nutcracker; twisted weltings, narrow braids, and leather lacings work well for ties.

Choose bright white, tan, or an unexpected color for Santa's trim; marabou feather boas are available in a variety of colors at fabric and costume supply stores. Select from a wide variety of elegant or casual trims, such as laces, medallions, beads, and buttons, for the Nutcracker's boot; stitch narrow trims side by side, or layer them on top of wider trims, if desired.

To avoid crushing the pile when sewing on velveteen or corduroy, use a walking foot, if you have one, and press the seams lightly. Stitch the feather trim to Santa's boot by hand, using a whipstitch, or by machine, using a piping foot and a long straight stitch.

MATERIALS

* ¾ yd. (0.7 m) fabric, for lining.
* ¾ yd. (0.7 m) low-loft batting.

For Santa's boot:

* ½ yd. (0.5 m) fabric, for boot and boot strap.
* ½ yd. (0.5 m) fabric, for pants leg and hanger.
* ½ yd. (0.5 m) marabou feather boa, for trim.
* Topstitching thread.
* 1½" (3.8 cm) buckle.

For Nutcracker's boot:

* ¾ yd. (0.7 m) fabric.
* ⅝ yd. (0.6 m) trim; glue stick, optional.
* Six ¾" to 1" (2 to 2.5 cm) buttons and ¾ yd. (0.7 m) narrow trim or lacing, or three frogs.
* Embellishments as desired.

CUTTING DIRECTIONS

For the Santa boot stocking, cut two Santa boots, using the pattern on page 122; clip at the marks. Cut a 3½" × 4½" (9 × 11.5 cm) rectangle, for the boot strap. Cut two pants legs, using the pattern on page 123.

For the Nutcracker stocking, cut two stockings, using the pattern on page 122.

For either style, cut two stockings from the lining and two from the batting, using the pattern on page 122; clip the lining at the marks. Cut one 2" × 6" (5 × 15 cm) rectangle, for the hanger.

HOW TO MAKE A SANTA'S BOOT

1 Stitch boot to pants leg, right sides together, using ½" (1.3 cm) seam allowance, for front. Press seam open. On right side, zigzag over topstitching thread ⅜" (1 cm) from pants-leg sides. Avoid piercing thread with needle; leave thread tails. Stitch boa over seam; trim boa at cut edge. Repeat, for back.

(Continued)

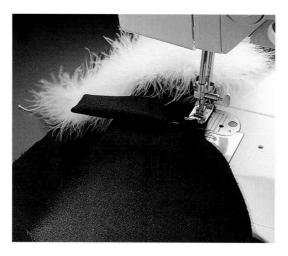

2 Fold boot strap in half lengthwise, right sides together. Stitch across short end and along side, using ¼" (6 mm) seam allowance. Trim corner; turn and press flat. Pin open end to edge of one boot, between clip marks; baste a scant ½" (1.3 cm) from cut edges.

3 Fold hanger in half lengthwise, right sides together. Stitch long side, using ¼" (6 mm) seam allowance; turn and press. Pin folded hanger to right side of back pants leg so ends align to upper edge, 1" (2.5 cm) from back side.

4 Pin front stocking to batting along boot edges and ½" (1.3 cm) from top; secure upper thread tails to top pins. Pull lower tails, gathering pants-leg sides to fit batting. Baste a scant ½" (1.3 cm) around stocking. Repeat, for back.

HOW TO MAKE A NUTCRACKER'S BOOT

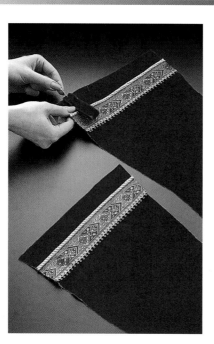

1 Position trims as desired on stocking front; cut trims even with stocking edges. Secure trims on stocking, using pins or glue stick; stitch along sides or through trim center as desired. Repeat on stocking back. Make and secure hanger to back as in step 3, above.

2 Pin stocking front to batting, right side up; baste a scant ½" (1.3 cm) around stocking. Repeat, for back. Follow steps 5 and 6, opposite, to line stocking. Position lining in stocking. Stitch buttons 1½" (3.8 cm) from seam, or stitch frogs across seam; avoid catching more than one layer of lining.

5 Stitch lining to stocking at upper edge, right sides together; use ½" (1.3 cm) seam allowance. Trim batting from seam allowance; press seam allowance toward lining. Edgestitch close to seam, securing lining to seam allowance.

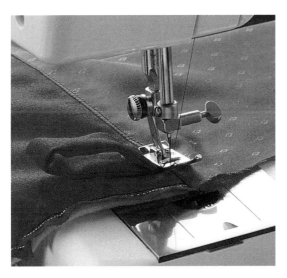

7 Position lining in stocking. Stitch buckle at desired location; avoid catching more than one layer of lining. Slip boot strap through buckle.

6 Pin front to back, right sides together; pin boot to boot and lining to lining. Stitch around stocking, using ½" (1.3 cm) seam allowance; leave opening in lining, between marks. Trim batting from seam allowance; clip curves, and turn right side out. Slipstitch opening closed.

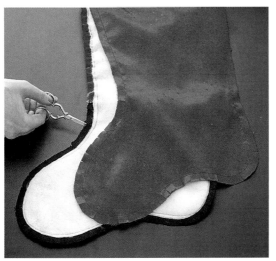

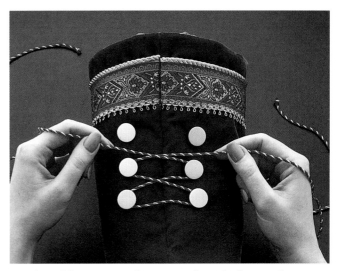

For chained buttons, cut three 6½" (16.3 cm) pieces of narrow trim or lacing. Tape ends of each piece together, forming three loops. Place loops around button sets; bend tape around back buttons.

For laced buttons, tie knot at each end of trim. Place trim center at seam between lower button set; wrap trim around buttons on alternating sides, wrapping to top set. Tie bow above top buttons.

MANTEL CLOTH

Create a beautiful mantel cloth to make your fireplace more festive. Outline the cloth with a twisted welting, suspend special ornaments at the front, and quilt holiday motifs or gentle swirls on the panels.

Develop the pattern pieces before purchasing fabric; you will want to railroad the fabric if the mantel length is longer than the fabric width to avoid seams in the mantel cloth. Measure patterns to determine yardage for cording or piping.

Select mediumweight fabrics and trims that coordinate with the rest of your holiday decorating. Calicos or textured linens, casual cotton welting, and wood or tin ornaments provide a casual or country feeling. Velvets, taffetas, or damasks, rayon welting, and crystal or polished metal ornaments are very elegant.

Choose a quilting motif that repeats or complements the ornaments; trace around cookie cutters or paper patterns. Use a walking foot to ease feeding of multiple fabric layers, if available. Or drop the feed dogs and stipple-quilt the panels; use an all-over, free-form design or fill in a motif's background.

Use at least four drapery weights to keep the top panel against the wall; you may choose to use more if your mantel is more than 45" (115 cm) long, if you design drops longer than the mantel depth, or to counter-balance heavy ornaments.

MATERIALS

* Paper, to make pattern; flexible curve, optional.
* Decorative fabric.
* Muslin.
* Batting.
* Lining fabric.
* Ribbon, 1/8" to 1/4" (3 to 6 mm) wide.
* Decorative twisted welting; transparent tape.
* Safety pins.
* Drapery weights, four or more.
* Ornaments; one for each upper point.
* 1/2" (1.3 cm) buttons; one for each ornament.

CUTTING DIRECTIONS

Cut three mantel fronts, using the pattern developed in steps 1 and 2; cut one each from fabric, batting, and lining. Cut six mantel sides, using the pattern developed in step 3; cut two each from fabric, batting, and lining. Cut three rectangles for the mantel top, with the length equal to the mantel length plus ½" (1.3 cm) of ease for every yard (meter) of length, and the width equal to the mantel depth; cut one each from fabric, batting, and lining.

Measure around the pattern pieces to determine the welting yardage; purchase an amount equal to the circumference of the front and side panels plus 6" (15 cm).

Determine the desired drop of the ornaments; cut one ribbon for each ornament equal to two times the drop plus 2" (5 cm).

HOW TO MAKE A MANTEL CLOTH

1 Measure mantel length; draw line on paper to this length plus ½" (1.3 cm) per yard (meter). Determine spacing of front points; divide length by desired number of points. Use perpendicular lines to mark location of each front point. Draw short dotted lines midway between perpendicular lines as shown.

(Continued)

2 Measure mantel height to determine minimum drop; mark this distance along dotted lines. Determine desired mantel drop at long points; mark this distance along solid lines. Draw front drop edge, using flexible curve, if desired. Add ½" (1.3 cm) seam allowances to all edges.

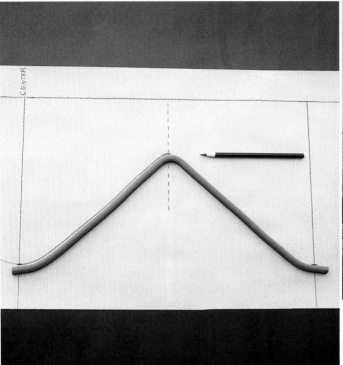

3 For side, draw rectangle with width equal to mantel depth and length equal to desired side drop. Shape drop as desired. Add ½" (1.3 cm) seam allowances to all edges. Cut out pattern pieces; tape to mantel to check size, proportion, and shape.

4 Mark quilting design on right side of front, using fabric pencil. Place front panel over front batting, right side up. Align all edges; pin. Machine-baste around panel. Repeat with side panels and top.

5 Identify right side of decorative welting; inner edge of tape is not visible on right side. Align welting to sides and front edge of top panel, right sides up, with cord along seamline; baste scant ½" (1.3 cm) from edges, using zipper foot. Clip tape to ease welting at corners and curves. Wrap transparent tape around ends to prevent raveling. Repeat with front and side panels, aligning welting to side and lower edges.

6 Place front over front lining, right sides together; pin all edges. Stitch sides and lower edge, using ½" (1.3 cm) seam allowances; use zipper foot, crowding welting. Trim batting from seam allowances; trim corners, and clip curves. Repeat for side panels.

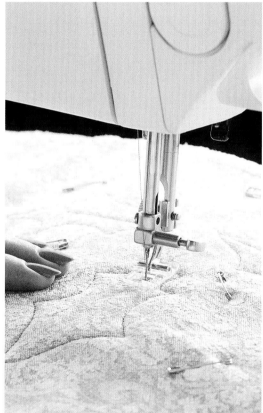

7 Turn pieces right side out; press lightly. Pin-baste around marked designs or at 3" (7.5 cm) intervals as desired. Stitch quilting designs as desired.

8 Pin side panels to top, right sides together, so side welting is ½" (1.3 cm) from long cut edges of top. Stitch, using zipper foot; crowd welting. Repeat, stitching front panel along front edge of top; welting of front and side panels should meet at corners.

(Continued)

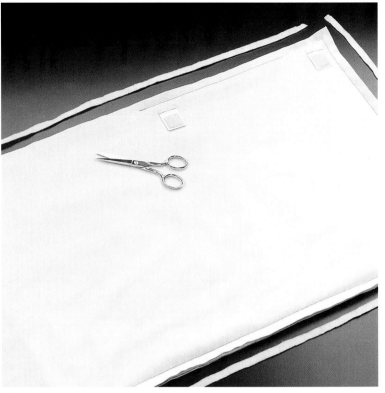

9 Attach drapery weights to wrong side of top lining, ⅝" to ¾" (1.5 to 2 cm) from one long edge. Secure one near each corner and two near center; secure more, if desired.

10 Place top lining on top, right sides together, so weights are at back; pin raw edges, carefully enclosing front and side panels. Stitch around top, using ½" (1.3 cm) seam allowances. Use zipper foot, crowding welting. Avoid catching panels in seams. Leave 6" (15 cm) opening on back edge. Trim batting from seam allowances; trim ½" (1.3 cm) at opening. Trim corners. Turn right side out and press lightly. Slipstitch opening closed. Stitch quilting design, if desired.

11 Stitch button to front panel lining and batting at each upper point, just above welting. Avoid catching front panel in stitches. Slip ribbon through ornament. Tie knot a distance from ornament equal to desired drop; tie second knot ⅝" (1.5 cm) from first knot. Repeat with each ornament. Attach ornaments at buttons, slipping button between knots.

ADVENT WREATH

This Advent wreath provides a unique way to share the joy of expectation all season long. Decorate a natural or artificial wreath to recall special memories, and open one small gift each day as you count down to Christmas.

Suspend a group of favorite mementos from the top of the wreath, and add embellishments that develop a favorite holiday theme. Cluster small embellishments on the top and sides to create an attractive flow for the eye; small bells or sturdy floral stems, such as mountain ash berries, work well and are available in several natural colors.

Purchase small, plain envelopes in stationery stores, or make your own envelopes using decorative or holiday wrapping papers. Number an envelope for each day; use a decorative pen, or select letter transfer sheets from assorted styles available at art and stationery stores.

Into the daily envelopes, slip coupons that may be exchanged immediately or throughout the coming year. Consider a small treat, a special privilege, or a day off from a specific chore; design them to please your family. Or purchase small, flat gifts, such as foil-wrapped candy coins or charms.

MATERIALS

* Wreath, 36" (91.5 cm) in diameter.
* Clusters of small embellishments or berry stems.
* Paddle floral wire; wire cutter.
* One to three large ornaments.
* Small embellishments, such as berries.
* 1 yd. (0.95 m) ribbon, 3" (7.5 cm) wide.
* 7¾ yds. (7.1 m) ribbon, ¼" to ½" (6 mm to 1.3 cm) wide.
* Twenty-five envelopes, 2" (5 cm) square, or decorative papers to make envelopes.
* Decorative pen or transfer letters, ½" (1.3 cm) tall, and stylus or craft stick.
* Glue stick; paper punch.
* Twenty-five small gifts.

1 Secure clustered embellishments to wreath frame at center top, using floral wire; bend stems or secure more clusters to follow upper curve of wreath. Allow an unadorned arc to remain bare at bottom; arrange needles to partially cover floral stems, if used.

2 Suspend large ornaments at center top, using narrow ribbon. Secure small embellishments as desired.

3 Tie bow in wide ribbon. Secure bow to wreath, just above ornaments, using wire; arrange and trim tails as desired. Cut narrow ribbon into twenty-five 11" (28 cm) lengths. Secure ribbons randomly over wreath surface, using wire; allow at least 2" (5 cm) between ribbons. If using purchased envelopes, omit step 4.

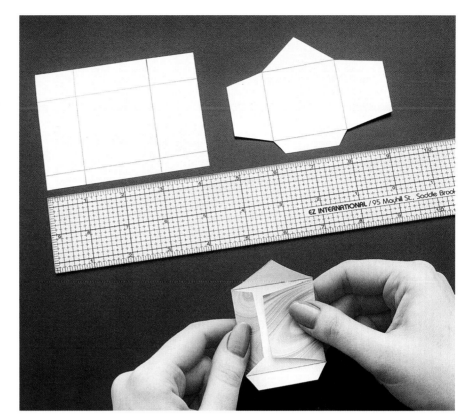

4 Cut 4¼" × 3¼" (10.8 × 8.2 cm) rectangle from decorative paper. Mark foldlines on wrong side of paper, 1" (2.5 cm) from one short side and 1¼" (3.2 cm) from other short side, ⅞" (2.2 cm) from top and ⅜" (1 cm) from bottom. Score foldlines, using table knife, if paper is heavy. Cut out four corners; shape flaps slightly, as shown. Fold envelope; secure narrow side over wide side and bottom flap over sides, using glue stick. Repeat to make twenty-five envelopes.

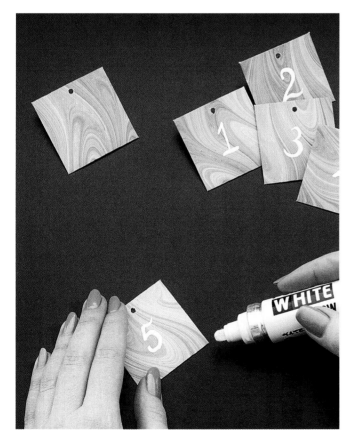

5 Label envelopes with numbers 1 through 25, using decorative pen. Or, position transfer sheet over each envelope, placing number near envelope center; rub number, using stylus or craft stick. Gently lift transfer sheet to ensure complete transfer.

6 Punch hole at tops of envelopes, using paper punch. Insert coupon or small flat gift in each envelope. Tie envelopes to wreath, using ribbons; arrange numbers randomly to avoid lopsided arrangement as envelopes are removed. Hang wreath, using wire loop on back.

ADVENT CALENDAR

This unique Advent calendar provides a visual reminder of your family's favorite holiday cookies. Create twenty-five polymer clay cookies, and count down to Christmas by hanging them on a beribboned baking sheet. Beginning December first, add one cookie each day until all are hanging on Christmas Day. Store the waiting cookies in a small cookie jar or mixing bowl.

Warm polymer clay to make it pliable; roll it between your palms, fold, and reroll until it is soft. Roll soft clay into a ball to eliminate bubbles before forming cookie shapes. Flatten balls slightly to make the simplest designs, like thumbprint cookies or a peanut butter kiss. Discover easy ways to duplicate other cookies in the tips, below. Refer to cookbooks for inspiration, or purchase holiday candy molds. Use disposable towelettes to clean your hands before working with another clay color.

Choose from a wide variety of traditional cookie decorations, including colored sugars, sprinkles, dots, and metallic balls; use baker's decorations that will not melt. Bake decorated shapes on a baking sheet, following the clay manufacturer's directions. Paint the cooled clay, if desired.

MATERIALS

* Polymer clay, assorted colors.
* Small Christmas cookie cutters; large dowel; Mylar® sheet.
* Candy molds; baby powder; small soft paintbrush; acrylic paints, optional.
* Decorative baker's toppings.
* Disposable towelettes; mat knife; toothpick; small dowel.
* Baking sheet, for baking clay.
* Acrylic spray sealer.
* Magnetic strip, ½" or 1" (1.3 or 2.5 cm) wide; scissors; all-purpose glue.
* Steel baking sheet, at least 17" × 11" (43 × 28 cm), with hole at one end; avoid the nonstick variety or the lower bow may not adhere well.
* Masking tape; permanent marker in desired color.
* ⅜ yd. (0.35 m) satin ribbon, ¼" (6 mm) wide.
* 4 yd. (3.7 m) reversible wired ribbon; 24- or 26-gauge wire.
* Hot glue gun.

TIPS FOR MAKING CLAY COOKIES

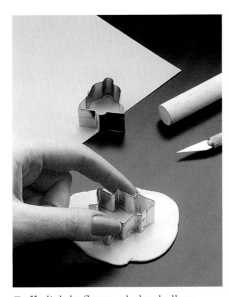

Roll slightly flattened clay ball on clean, smooth surface to about ³⁄₁₆" (4.5 mm), using Mylar sheet between clay and dowel. Use cookie cutters or knife to cut designs. Lift clay shapes using knife, if necessary.

Form rods by rolling ball on surface with fingers; avoid thick and thin areas by moving hands over full length. Place thick rods side by side, and twist gently for candy canes; place medium rods side by side, and spiral length around one end for pinwheels.

Dust candy mold with small amount of baby powder, using brush. Warm clay to fill mold about halfway; press ball into general shape, and push into mold. Insert toothpick gently at edge where design shows a dent or inner angle; gently pry clay from mold.

(Continued)

Decorate cookies as desired. Cut or pinch layered details from thin sheets. Arrange and gently press thin rods on cookie to imitate frosting. Shape small clay balls into chocolate kisses, cinnamon bits, or other candies as desired. Roll tiny clay balls or use decorative baker's toppings for additional color and detail; press small parts gently into clay to secure.

Use toothpick or small dowel to smooth edges and improve bond between colors. Use sharp tips or flat ends to add surface details or natural texture.

Paint details on cured and cooled cookies, if desired. Glue small decorations in place, if necessary. Spray cookies with acrylic sealer; allow to dry thoroughly.

Cut magnet strip as long as possible, so the weight of the cookie will not cause it to slip; trim width, if necessary, so strip is not visible from front. Glue to back of cookie, using an all-purpose glue; allow glue to cure as manufacturer directs.

HOW TO MAKE AN ADVENT CALENDAR

1 Plan placement of numbers on sheet, using tape; alternate four rows of four and three rows of three, as shown below. Write numbers 1 through 25 on baking sheet, using permanent marker; begin with 25 in the upper left corner.

2 Fold satin ribbon in half; pass fold through hole in end of baking sheet, and slip ends through loop, drawing tight. Knot ribbon about 2½" (6.5 cm) from sheet; tie bow over knot.

3 Cut 1½ yd. (1.4 m) length from wired ribbon. Wrap ribbon over thumb for center loop; form loop on each side. Form slightly larger loop on each side. Insert wire through center loop. Bend wire around ribbon; twist wire tightly, gathering ribbon. Secure wire to baking sheet at hole; trim excess wire. Shape ribbon loops; trim tails, if desired.

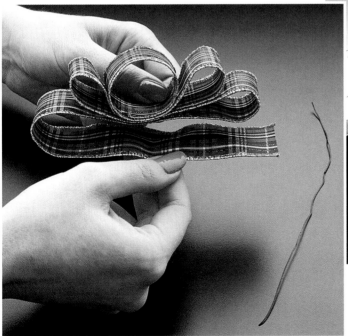

4 Make bow with tails, using remaining wired ribbon. Form three loops on each side of center loop, and secure loops with wire, as in step 3. Trim tails as desired. Glue bow to center bottom of baking sheet, using hot glue.

PATCHWORK SANTA WALL QUILT

This three-dimensional Santa wall quilt has a button mouth, wire spectacles, a big round nose, and a jingle bell dangling from the tip of his hat, just like the patchwork Santa tree skirt (page 48). Piece three jolly Santa faces, following the general directions for the skirt, and join them with a merry Ho! Ho! Ho!

Quilt the layered top minimally by stitching around the lettering and along the outer block, sashing, and border seamlines. Or quilt the top more fully by stitching within areas; stitch small snowflakes in the air behind Santa, quilt Christmas designs in the borders, or stitch around printed designs in the fabric.

MATERIALS

* ⅛ yd. (0.15 m) fabric, for face and nose.
* ¼ yd. (0.25 m) white faux fur, for beard and hat trim.
* ⅓ yd. (0.32 m) red fabric, for hat, corners, and letters.
* ¼ yd. (0.25 m) light or off-white fabric, for corners.
* 1 yd. (0.95 m) green fabric, for background, sashing, and borders.
* ¾ yd. (0.7 m) coordinating fabric, for quilt back.
* 27" × 45" (68.5 × 115 cm) quilt batting.
* Three ⅝" (1.5 cm) red buttons, for mouths.
* Three brass jingle bells, ½" (1.3 cm) or 15 mm.
* 1 yd. (0.95 m) 24-gauge brass wire, for glasses.
* Polyester fiberfill.
* Blush; black fabric paint or permanent marker or embroidery floss.
* Masking tape; safety pins; quilter's pencil, optional.
* 1⅔ yd. (1.58 m) ribbon, ¼" (6 mm) wide, for hanger loops and bows.
* One 24" (61 cm) cafe curtain rod, brass finish.
* ¾ yd. (0.7 m) decorative cord, for hanger.
* One decorative wall hanger, brass finish.

CUTTING DIRECTIONS

Cut one 1½" (3.8 cm) strip from the face fabric, using a straight-edge and rotary cutter. Cut quadrilaterals, as shown on page 50, so the sides measure 12½" (31.8 cm) and 9½" (24.3 cm); repeat twice to cut three faces.

Draw a 3" (7.5 cm) diameter circle on paper; use it as a pattern to cut three noses.

Cut one 2" (5 cm) strip of faux fur. Cut a quadrilateral, as shown on page 50, so the sides measure 10½" (26.8 cm) and 6½" (16.3 cm); repeat twice to cut three hat brims.

Cut two 9" (23 cm) squares from faux fur. Cut them in half diagonally for three beards; discard one. Or, if the fur has a nap, make a pattern first. Cut the beards so the fur brushes toward the lower point.

Cut two 5½" (14 cm) squares from the red fabric; stack the squares. Cut them in half diagonally for three hats; discard one.

Trace the pattern (page 119) for the hat tip, and cut three from the red fabric.

Cut three 6½" (16.3 cm) squares from the red fabric; stack and cut them diagonally, for six corner pieces.

Cut three 6½" (16.3 cm) squares from the light or off-white fabric; stack them and cut diagonally, for six corner pieces.

Cut three 11¾" × 8" (30 × 20.5 cm) rectangles from the green fabric. Also cut four 2¾" × 19¼" (7 × 48.1 cm) strips, for the sashing and borders. Cut two 2¾" × 43¼" (7 × 110 cm) strips, for the side borders. Cut four 2½" (6.5 cm) strips across the width of the fabric, for the binding.

Cut the ribbon into five 3" (7.5 cm) lengths and five 9" (23 cm) lengths.

1 Make three Santa blocks, as on pages 51 and 52, steps 1 to 5. Stitch light background corners to upper sides of blocks and red background corners to lower sides of blocks, right sides together, keeping jingle bell tip free. Press seam allowances toward corners.

2 Enlarge, trace, cut, and apply one set of HO! letters to each green rectangle, as on page 53, step 2; arrange letters as shown.

(Continued)

3 Align rectangle that reads on an upward diagonal to left side of Santa block, right sides together; stitch. Repeat, aligning two downward diagonals to right side of remaining blocks. Press seam allowances toward rectangles. Arrange sashing and short border strips above and below Santa rectangles; stitch, right sides together, to make top as shown.

4 Stitch side borders to pieced top, right sides together. Press seam allowances toward sashing and borders. Mark additional quilting design, if desired, using quilting pencil lightly.

5 Tape backing to work surface, wrong side up, so it is taut, but not stretched. Smooth batting over backing. Center quilt top over batting, right side up; smooth.

6 Baste layers together using safety pins, working from center of quilt to sides; avoid pinning along seams. Remove tape from backing. Fold edges of backing over edges of quilt top; pin-baste.

7 Stitch in the ditch around Santa blocks and along all corner, sashing, and border seams; stitch from center to edges. Stitch close to edges of all fused letters. Stitch additional quilting designs, if desired. Remove pins.

8 Measure quilt top across middle; trim binding strip to this measurement. Press binding strip in half lengthwise, wrong sides together. Pin strip to upper edge of quilt top, matching raw edges; ease fullness as necessary. Stitch binding strip to quilt, using scant 1/4" (6 mm) seam allowance. Trim excess batting and backing to a scant 1/2" (1.3 cm) from the stitching. Repeat at the lower edge.

9 Wrap binding strip snugly around edge of quilt, covering stitching line on back; pin in the ditch of the seam. Stitch in the ditch on right side of quilt, catching binding on back.

10 Repeat steps 8 and 9 for quilt sides, measuring quilt top down center and trimming strips to measurement plus 1" (2.5 cm), for 1/2" (1.3 cm) extensions at top and bottom. Fold extensions over finished edges before final pinning.

11 Complete Santa blocks, as on pages 52 and 53, steps 6 to 8. Fold 3" (7.5 cm) ribbon to form loop, and stitch ends securely to upper corner of quilt. Form small bow, using 9" (23 cm) ribbon; hand-stitch over loop, hiding ends. Repeat at opposite corner; space three more loops and bows evenly across upper edge. Insert cafe rod through loops. Attach cord to rod ends; hang on decorative wall hook.

SHAPED &
TASSELED PILLOWS

Tuck these fun holiday-shaped pillows in surprising places to add a festive touch throughout the house, or add them to an existing pillow collection.

Select fabrics that reflect the shapes themselves, according to your own style. Add tassels to the corners of the tree pillow, and outline the star with a decorative cord. Use novelty or jeweled buttons and beads for more ornaments and added starlight, if desired.

MATERIALS

* Paper, for pattern; straightedge; fabric pencil.
* Polyester fiberfill.
* Fusible interfacing to back lightweight fabrics.
* ⅓ yd. (0.32 m) fabric, for tree center.
* ¼ yd. (0.25 m) contrasting fabric, for tree border.
* 4½" × 2" (11.5 × 5 cm) fabric piece, for tree trunk.
* Three tassels, for tree.
* ½ yd. (0.5 m) fabric, for star.
* 1½ yd. (1.4 m) decorative cord, ¼" (6 mm) wide, for star; liquid fray preventer.
* Buttons and beads, optional.

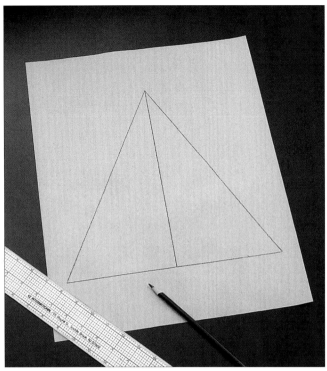

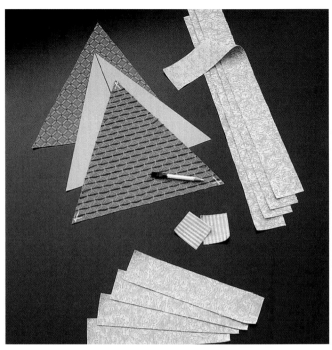

1 Draw 12" (30.5 cm) line on paper; mark center. Draw 11" (28 cm) perpendicular line, starting at center; draw lines from each end of first line to top of second line, forming triangle, for pattern.

2 Cut two fabric triangles, using pattern. Cut six 2¼" × 20" (6 × 51 cm) strips for border; cut two strips in half, crosswise. Cut two 2¼" × 2" (6 × 5 cm) pieces for trunk. Fuse interfacing to wrong side of lightweight fabrics. Mark each point on wrong side of triangles where ¼" (6 mm) seams meet.

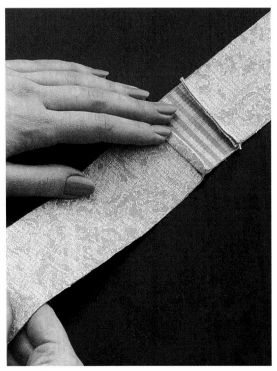

3 Stitch short strips to short sides of trunk piece, right sides together; finger-press seams toward trunk. Repeat for second trunk strip.

4 Center short triangle side on trunk strip, right sides together, and pin; strip will extend beyond triangle ends. Stitch ¼" (6 mm) seam between marked points, backstitching at each point. Stitch plain strips to adjacent sides, keeping strips free from new seams. Repeat, for back.

5 Fold triangle in half through one point, right sides together, aligning strip edges. Position straightedge along fold, as shown; mark line on strip, using fabric pencil. Stitch on line, backstitching at seam intersection. Repeat at remaining corners. Trim excess fabric. Repeat, for back. Carefully press seam allowances to one side; avoid distorting triangles.

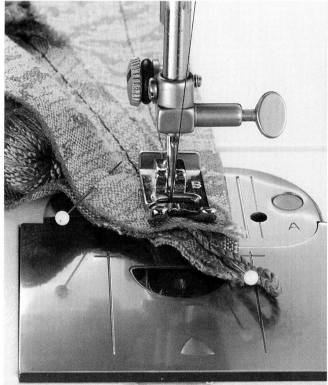

7 Stuff pillow with fiberfill. Slipstitch opening closed. Add embellishments as desired.

6 Pin tassels at corners of back; part of cord will extend beyond cut edges. Pin pillow front to back, right sides together; stitch, using ½" (1.3 cm) seam allowances. Leave 5" (12.5 cm) opening on bottom. Trim corners, and press seam allowances open; turn right side out.

HOW TO MAKE A STAR PILLOW

1 Draw an 18" (46 cm) diameter circle on paper, using string tied to a pencil. Divide circle into five parts; marks should be about 11⅜" (29 cm) apart.

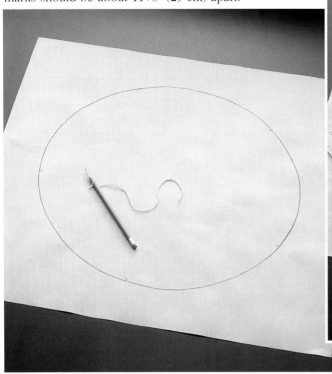

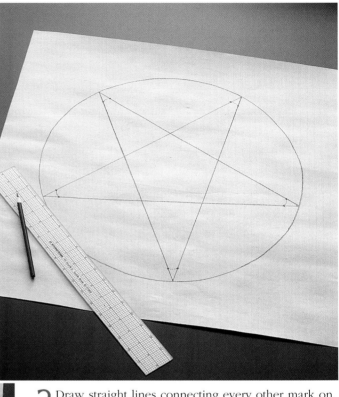

2 Draw straight lines connecting every other mark on circle. Round off star points 1" (2.5 cm) from ends.

3 Cut two stars from fabric, using pattern. Fuse interfacing to wrong side of lightweight fabrics. Pin stars right sides together, aligning edges. Stitch, using ¼" (6 mm) seam allowance; take short stitch across each point. Leave 3" (7.5 cm) opening on one side. Clip into each corner; trim points. Press seam allowances open; turn.

4 Stuff pillow with fiberfill; use pencil to pack fiberfill into points. Slipstitch opening closed.

5 Seal cord end with liquid fray preventer; allow to dry. Trim end clean. Whipstitch cord over seam, starting at inner corner. Seal cord where it meets end; trim clean when dry, and secure with hand stitches.

PILLOW CHANGERS

Dress up your everyday knife-edge pillows with these holiday ideas. Select fabrics that complement the pillows you wish to cover and that blend well with your home's decor.

Design pillow toppers to cover one-third to two-thirds of the pillow, shaping the lower edge as you desire. Embellish them with beads, bells, buttons, and more.

Reverse colors for toppers and overlays on contrasting pillows, if desired.

Select from a variety of colors in fabrics such as organza and ninon to make a sheer, flanged overlay for your pillow; choose a similar tone for a subtle change, or use a contrasting color for greater interest.

MATERIALS

* Paper, to draw pattern for topper.

* Fabric, for topper; ½ yd. (0.5 m) for toppers covering the upper third of pillows up to 20" (51 cm) square; ¾ yd. (0.7 m) for longer toppers.

* Sheer fabric, for overlay; pillows up to 14" (35.5 cm) square require only ⅝ yd. (0.6 m).

* Embellishments as desired.

CUTTING DIRECTIONS

For a topper, cut four pieces, using the pattern as drawn in steps 1 and 2.

For an overlay, cut one rectangle with the length equal to the pillow height plus 5" (12.5 cm) and the width equal to two times the pillow width plus 14" (35.5 cm).

HOW TO MAKE A PILLOW TOPPER

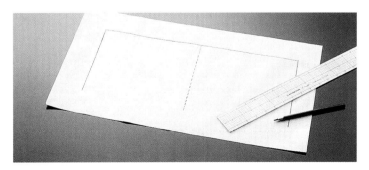

1 Measure pillow width, including trim; draw line on paper equal to this length plus ½" (1.3 cm). Draw perpendicular lines at each end that are at least one-third the pillow height; draw dotted line at center.

(Continued)

2 Draw desired hem shape; draw from one side to dotted line for symmetrical hem. Add ½" (1.3 cm) seam allowance to all sides. If symmetrical, fold on dotted line; cut on outer lines.

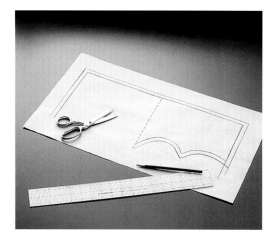

3 Align sides and upper edge of two pieces, right sides together, and stitch, using ½" (1.3 cm) seam allowance; leave hem open. Trim corners; press seam allowances open.

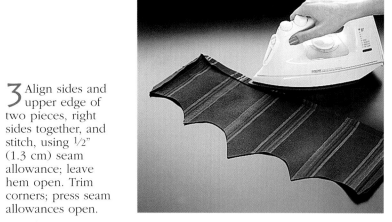

4 Repeat step 3 with remaining two pieces, for lining, using ½" (1.3 cm) seam allowance on sides and ⅝" (1.5 cm) seam allowance along upper edge; leave 5" (12.5 cm) opening along upper edge.

HOW TO MAKE A SHEER FLANGED OVERLAY

1 Press under ¾" (2 cm) double hem on each short end; stitch close to inner fold. Mark long sides at center and points 1½" (3.8 cm) from ends, using pins. Fold end marks to center mark, wrong sides together, so hems overlap 3" (7.5 cm); pin.

5 Add tassels at hem edge, as on page 108, step 2, if desired. Align seams and hem edges of topper and lining, right sides together; pin. Stitch, using ½" (1.3 cm) seam allowance. Trim points; clip curves. Turn right side out through opening; press.

6 Slipstitch opening closed. Hand-stitch any bells, beads, or decorative buttons. Place topper over upper edge of pillow.

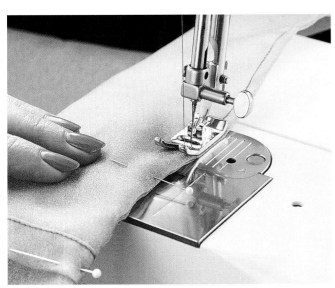

2 Stitch seams, using short stitches and ¼" (6 mm) seam allowances. Trim seams, using pinking shears, if possible. Turn wrong side out; press seam edges. Stitch again ¼" (6 mm) from edges.

3 Turn right side out; press. Stitch around entire pillow cover, 2" (5 cm) from edge; use tape strip on machine bed as stitching guide, if desired. Insert pillow.

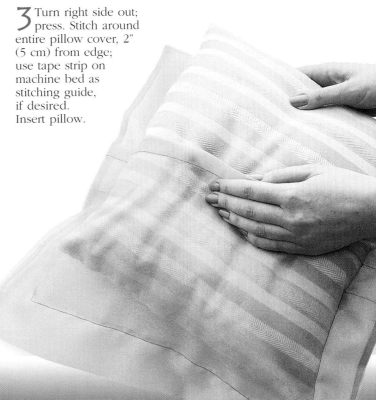

SANTA'S PILLOW COLLECTION

Piece a merry Santa face, convert an everyday pillow into his hefty sack, and wrap an ordinary pillow to look like a gift. Set the three pillows together as a reminder of holiday folklore, or use the ideas separately for a simple decorative touch.

Choose fabrics used elsewhere in your home or select all new for a coordinated set. Use fabrics that reflect your personal style; make them elegant in velvet and satin, or casual in a coarsely textured linen, hopsacking, or calico. Select a non-directional print for the sack. Tie the sack simply with a knotted cord, or make matching ribbon bows for both the sack and gift.

MATERIALS

* Fabrics for Santa's face, nose, beard, and hat;
  ½ yd. (0.5 m) fabric for border and pillow
  back; 14" (35.5 cm) pillow form.

* Fabric for sack and gift; yardage will vary
  with pillow size.

* ½ to ¾ yd. (0.5 to 0.7 m) decorative cord,
  for knotted sack.

* 1 yd. (0.95 m) ribbon, for sack with bow.

* 1 to 3 yd. (0.95 to 2.75 m) ribbon, for gifts
  with bows, depending on pillow size.

CUTTING DIRECTIONS

For a Santa pillow, cut one face, nose, hat brim, beard, hat, and hat tip, following the general cutting directions on page 50. Cut two 3½" × 8½" (9 × 21.8 cm) strips and two 3½" × 15" (9 × 38 cm) strips from the border fabric. Cut one 15" (38 cm) square for the pillow back.

For Santa's sack, measure the pillow. For the sack, cut a rectangle with the height equal to three-and-one-half times the pillow height and the width equal to the pillow width plus 2" (5 cm). Cut a rectangle for the lining with the height equal to the pillow height plus 2" (5 cm) and the width equal to twice the pillow width plus 3" (7.5 cm).

To wrap a pillow, cut a rectangle with the height equal to two times the pillow height plus 9" (23 cm) and the width equal to the pillow width plus 9" (23 cm).

HOW TO MAKE A SANTA PILLOW

1 Make one Santa block, as on pages 51 and 52, steps 1 to 5. Align short border strips to opposite sides of block, right sides together; stitch, using ¼" (6 mm) seam allowances. Stitch long border strips to remaining opposite sides of block, right sides together; press seam allowances toward borders. Complete pillow as on page 79, steps 6 and 7; use pillow form and omit reference to tassels. Complete Santa block as on page 52, steps 6 to 8.

HOW TO GIFT WRAP A PILLOW

1 Press under ⅜" (1 cm) on each side of fabric. Unfold corner; fold diagonally so pressed folds match. Press the diagonal fold; trim corner as shown. Repeat at each corner.

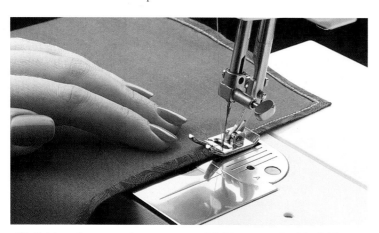

2 Fold under raw edges to pressed folds; press double-fold hems in place. Stitch around rectangle close to inner fold.

3 Place pillow on wrong side of fabric; wrap as you would a gift, securing flaps with safety pins. Wrap ribbon around pillow as desired, hiding pins; adjust pin location, if necessary.

HOW TO MAKE SANTA'S SACK

1 Fold sack fabric in half, crosswise; pin sides. Stitch, using ½" (1.3 cm) seam allowance. Trim corners. Pin short ends of lining together; stitch to form circle. Press seams open. Finish lower edge of lining, if desired.

2 Place lining in sack, right sides together, matching lining seam to side seam; pin upper edges. Stitch, using ½" (1.3 cm) seam allowance; press seam allowance open.

4 Turn sack right side out; insert pillow. Tie sack closed above pillow, using decorative cord or ribbon.

3 Turn lining down over wrong side of sack. Tack lining to sack at seam allowances. Topstitch upper edge, if desired.

SHELL-TRIMMED CHRISTMAS TREE

Collecting colorful shells and bits of sea life entrances children of all ages, and this miniature Christmas tree displays the smallest treasures beautifully.

Find small trees in gift and Christmas shops. Discover shells and colorful bits of coral while exploring the ocean beach or in nature shops.

Make a glue paste to ease shell positioning without sliding and to shorten setting times; it's very child friendly! Just pour white craft glue into a small container, and stir occasionally until thick.

MATERIALS

Miniature trees.

Wire cutter; white acrylic paint; fine glitter, optional.

Paste of condensed craft glue; craft stick.

Tiny seashells and sea life bits.

Baby oil or mineral oil, optional.

HOW TO MAKE A SHELL-TRIMMED CHRISTMAS TREE

1 Separate connected tree branches, if necessary, using wire cutter. Paint tree base and branches; sprinkle fine glitter on wet paint, if desired. Examine all sides of shells and sea life bits. Select the most colorful pieces, planning at least one piece for each branch; separate by size and color strength.

2 Plan location of shells and bits on tree, spacing most colorful pieces evenly around tree; gradually increase size from top to bottom. Place small paste dollop on tip of branch; gently press colorful shell or bit on paste. Repeat with all colorful pieces; fill in with less colorful shells. Layer pieces as desired.

3 Position pointed shells so narrow ends point to tree trunk. Attach sea star at treetop with one leg pointing straight up.

4 Allow glue to dry thoroughly. Brush on light coat of baby oil or mineral oil, to restore color and sheen to well-worn or aged shells.

MR. & MRS. FROST

Mr. and Mrs. Frost are happy to be in from the cold. Set them by the fire or on a buffet table, or let them greet your guests near the front door. Mr. Frost stands about 14" (35.5 cm) tall; she's a little shorter.

Sew the bodies using snow-white cotton velour, terry cloth, or polar fleece. Create a carrot nose from a simple felt triangle. Use beads for their coal eyes and mouths; choose multifaceted beads to add a little twinkle. Dress them in country casual clothes; recycle an old pair of jeans to make his overalls, and select a small gingham check or tiny holiday print for his scarf and her apron.

Consider how you can use the jeans' features to add interest and imitate factory detailing. Use a tiny change

pocket or the manufacturer's label for the bib's pocket, or stitch it to the back of the pants. Secure a size label at the pocket's side, if desired. Select topstitching thread in a color to match the original topstitching, if possible. Save rivets; glue them to overalls as embellishment, if desired.

Purchase small buckets or baskets for Mr. and Mrs. Frost to carry; fill them with silk holly clusters, poinsettias, or red berries, available in floral and craft shops. Use additional small florals to embellish the apron and hats. Or make a tiny firewood tote from a scrap of fabric.

MATERIALS

* ½ yd. (0.5 m) fabric, for bodies and arms; safety pins.
* Polyester fiberfill.
* White pearl cotton, size 3.
* Four ¾" (2 cm) buttons, to secure arms; 5" (12.5 cm) doll needle.
* Orange felt scrap; orange or gold topstitching thread.
* Four ⅜" (1 cm) black beads, for eyes.
* Ten small black beads, for mouth.
* Cosmetic blush; craft glue.
* ⅜ yd. (0.35 m) fabric for scarf and apron.

For Mr. Frost:

* One pair worn jeans.
* Topstitching thread.
* Four ⅜" to ½" (1 to 1.3 cm) buttons, for overalls.
* Hat, about 6" (15 cm) in diameter.
* Embellishments as desired.

For Mrs. Frost:

* ⅝ yd. (0.6 m) eyelet trim, ¾" (2 cm) wide.
* Two ⅜" to ½" (1 to 1.3 cm) buttons, for apron.
* Hat, diameter will vary with style.
* Embellishments as desired.

CUTTING DIRECTIONS

Cut a felt rectangle 1½" × 3" (3.8 × 7.5 cm); cut it in half diagonally to make two noses.

For Mr Frost:

Cut two body pieces, using the pattern on pages 120 and 121; follow outer line. Mark the neck and waist with safety pins. Cut four arms, using the pattern on page 121.

Cut one 5¼" × 4" (13.2 × 10 cm) rectangle from the bottom of a jeans leg, for the front bib; include the hem on the long side. Cut one 2¾" × 2¼" (7 × 6 cm) rectangle, for a pocket, if desired. Cut two 1¼" × 9" (3.2 × 23 cm) strips, for the straps. Cut one 8" × 9½" (20.5 × 24.3 cm) rectangle, for the pants; center it over the jeans seam.

Cut a 10" (25.5) square of scarf fabric, then cut it in half diagonally, for the bandanna; discard one triangle. Or cut a 1¼" × 22" (3.2 × 56 cm) strip, for a muffler.

For Mrs. Frost:

Cut two body pieces, using the pattern on pages 120 and 121; follow inner line. Mark the neck and waist with safety pins. Cut four arms, using the pattern on page 121.

Cut a 12" × 3¼" (30.5 × 8.2 cm) rectangle, rounding the bottom corners, for the apron skirt. Cut a 2½" × 5" (6.5 × 12.5 cm) rectangle, for the bib. Cut a 1½" × 24" (3.8 × 61 cm) strip for the waist tie. Cut a 1½" × 9" (3.8 × 23 cm) strip, for the neck strap.

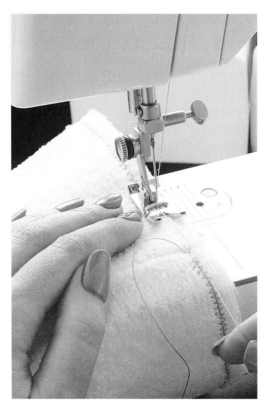

1 Align body pieces, right sides together; pin. Stitch, using ¼" (6 mm) seam allowance; leave bottom open. Zigzag over topstitching thread ⅜" (1 cm) from opening, right side up; avoid piercing thread with needle. Leave topstitching thread tails.

2 Stuff body to neck safety pin, using fiberfill; remove pin. Wrap neck tight, using pearl cotton. Push more fiberfill into head area, using eraser end of pencil, to make firm round head about 4½" (11.5 cm) wide.

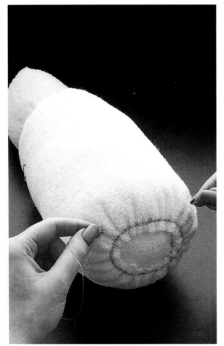

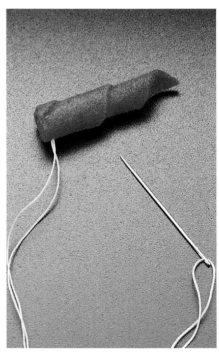

3 Stuff remaining body; place fabric scrap over fiberfill. Gather bottom, pulling thread tails; leave small opening. Wrap pearl cotton around body at waist pin, pulling in slightly; remove pin. Adjust location of waist, if desired; tack pearl cotton in place at center front and back.

4 Align two arm pieces, right sides together; pin. Stitch, using ¼" (6 mm) seam allowance; leave 1½" (3.8 cm) opening at upper back side. Stuff with fiberfill; slipstitch opening closed. Repeat for other arm. Stitch arms to body at desired location, using buttons, pearl cotton, and doll needle.

5 Thread long hand needle with 28" (71 cm) length of orange or gold thread; knot ends together. Roll felt triangle tightly from short side to narrow point; keep base even. Secure thread on base end; push needle through rolled felt at base.

6 Wrap thread around roll one-and-a-half times; take small stitch through roll. Wrap thread in opposite direction of first wrap. Continue until length is secure. Catching felt at tip, slip needle into roll at tip and come out at base; knot. Insert needle into head at desired nose location; gently squeeze head to bring needle out at back. Pull firmly to sink nose slightly into fabric; knot thread and trim tails.

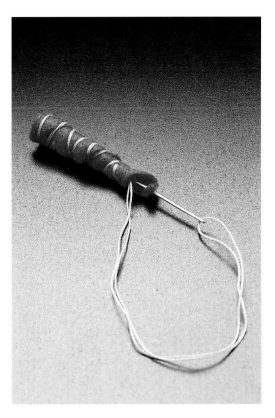

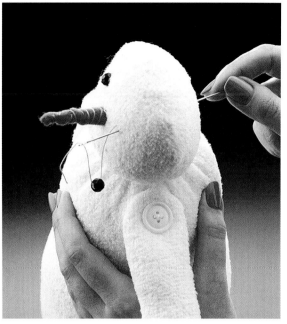

7 Sew large beads slightly above nose, for eyes, using doll needle; pull firmly to sink beads slightly into fabric. Knot at head back. Sew small beads below nose, for mouth. Apply cosmetic blush to cheeks lightly.

HOW TO DRESS MR. FROST

1 Turn under ½" (1.3 cm) on long sides of front bib; topstitch, using decorative thread, if desired. Turn under ⅜" (1 cm) on long sides of pocket, if using denim rectangle; repeat on short sides. Center pocket on bib just below original hemmed edge; pin. Topstitch pocket bottom and sides; stitch small triangles at upper corners for reinforcement stitching, if desired.

2 Pin short sides of pants rectangle right sides together; stitch, using ½" (1.3 cm) seam allowance. Press seam allowance open. Finish lower edge, if desired. Zigzag over topstitching thread ¼" (6 mm) from lower edge of pants, wrong side up; avoid piercing thread with needle. Leave topstitching thread tails. Pull tails to gather, leaving 1" (2.5 cm) opening; knot tails.

(Continued)

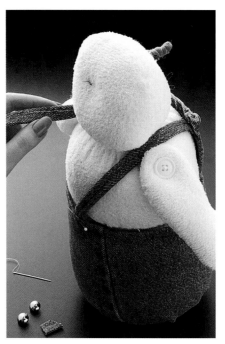

3 Turn pants right side out. Turn under ½" (1.3 cm) along upper edge. Pin pants to bibs, placing original pants seam at bib center; lap bib about ⅜" (1 cm). Topstitch upper pants edge, securing bib.

4 Turn under ⅜" (1 cm) on both long sides of straps; topstitch down center. Secure straps to upper corners of bib, using buttons. Insert body into pants; cross straps at center back. Trim straps ¾" (2 cm) below upper edge of pants; secure straps to pants, using buttons.

5 Wrap scarf around neck. Secure embellishments to hat as desired; set hat on head. Hand-stitch basket, bucket, or firewood tote to hand. Embellish further as desired.

HOW TO DRESS MRS. FROST

1 Lap eyelet trim binding over apron skirt sides and bottom; stitch. Baste upper edge; pull thread to gather edge to about 5" (12.5 cm). Fold bib in half crosswise, right sides together; stitch sides, using ¼" (6 mm) seam allowance. Turn; press flat. Stitch trim to upper edge of bib. Lap skirt upper edge over bib, matching centers; baste.

2 Fold waist tie in half lengthwise, right sides together. Stitch long side, using ¼" (6 mm) seam allowance. Turn; press flat. Repeat for neck strap. Lap waist tie over skirt upper edge, matching centers; topstitch to secure skirt, bib, and tie. Secure one neck strap end behind bib upper corner, using button. Position apron on body; tie waist at back. Wrap neck strap around neck; trim to desired length, and secure. Embellish as desired.

THE GUESTS ARE HERE!

Your friends have arrived in formal attire, but it's a little too warm inside for jackets and wraps. Make their bodies as for Mr. and Mrs. Frost and substitute a satin or moiré, if desired.

Recycle an old pair of dress slacks to create the gentleman's pants; use the pants hem at the waist to eliminate topstitching. Add satin ribbon tuxedo stripes down the legs, if desired. Purchase decorative ribbon or

braid for suspenders. Give him a bow tie of satin ribbon and a rayon frog cummerbund. Place a bottle of bubbly in his silver bucket. Add a ribbon muffler over his shoulders.

Use a slightly longer piece of satin, taffeta, or a sheer organdy for the lady's backless dress; finish the edges to prevent raveling. Select a decorative ribbon or lace to edge the dress.

This is the season for entertaining. Seasonal celebrations with family and friends are enhanced with heartfelt greetings and personalized gifts.

HAPPY
HOLIDAYS

Encourage the artist in the young and not-as-young when making cards that reflect holiday traditions. Use these simple one-of-a-kind works of art to greet friends far away or use them as party invitations, place cards, gift tags, ornaments, and thank-you notes.

Find design inspiration in holiday books, dishes, ornaments, and fabrics. Trace cookie cutters and stencils for the simplest cutout motifs. Tear papers for delightful deckle-edged designs. Mix and match the styling variations and enjoy making each unique card.

Select card stock or cover-weight papers at art and stationery stores. Discover unlimited choices for decorative papers, including solids, geometric or marbleized prints, papers with bits of glitter or pine, even wrapping papers and candy bar foils.

Mail cards in envelopes that meet postal regulations, available at stationery or paper supply stores.

MATERIALS

* Card stock or heavyweight stationery; scissors.
* Table knife; straightedge.
* Decorative paper as desired.
* Scissors with decorative-edge blades, optional.
* Spray adhesive or craft glue.
* Decorative pens, optional.
* Envelopes, optional.

For cut cards:

* Tracing paper, graphite paper, cookie cutters, optional.
* Mat knife; cutting surface.

HOW TO MAKE A CARD

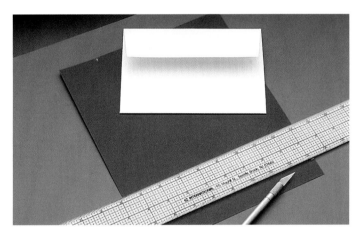

1 Subtract ¼" (6 mm) from envelope dimensions to determine the card size; decide location of opening. For side-opening card, cut card stock to determined height with twice the determined width. For bottom-opening card, cut card stock to determined width with twice the determined height.

2 Lightly mark wrong side of card at centers of sides to be folded, using pencil. Align straightedge at marks; score foldline, using table knife.

3 Create card design, using one of the methods below or opposite. Cut or tear decorative paper slightly smaller than card; use scissors with decorative-edge blades, if desired. Secure paper to inside of card, using adhesive; smooth out any bubbles. Write holiday message, using decorative pens, if desired.

HOW TO MAKE A CUTOUT CARD

1 Make card as on page 101, steps 1 and 2. Mark areas of card to be cut away on wrong side of card front, using graphite paper or tracing around cookie cutter. Mark mirror image of letters and directional designs.

2 Using mat knife, cut outline around the design, touching some of its outer edges to remove design background **(a),** or remove silhouette **(b)**. Fold card. Complete card, as on page 101, step 3.

HOW TO MAKE A TORN PAPER CARD

1 Make card as on page 101, steps 1 and 2. Tear general shapes of chosen design motif from colored papers; ignore small details to capture main features of shape. Arrange pieces on card; secure each piece, using glue. Complete card as on page 101, step 3.

CARD VARIATIONS

Fold card twice *so ends meet or lap.*

Use two papers on inside of card. *Cut or punch holes in front liner to reveal a design's second color— the back liner.*

Fold card front smaller than back (called a short fold). *Place part of the total design "inside."*

HOSTESS GIFTS: BOTTLES & JARS

W hen you give these unique hostess gifts, the lovely containers eliminate the need for further wrapping. Just decorate jars and bottles of food, oils, or wine to reflect the gift itself. Here are a few ideas to get you started.

Apple cider with cinnamon sticks. Secure a bundle of cinnamon sticks with a rubber band. Tie narrow ribbon over the band, adding a small ornament or holiday charm at the bow. Suspend the bundle on the side of a decorative bottle filled with apple cider, and tie a large bow around the neck.

Dressed-up wine. Attach a spray of gold holly, faux grapes, or berries to a bottle of wine, using wire. Hide the wire beneath a large velvet bow with tails.

Olive oil with pasta. Fill a tall, decorative bottle with olive oil. Secure a package of pasta to the side of the bottle, using large rubber bands. Tie wide decorative ribbon over the bands. Hang garlic bulbs or dried red peppers with jingle bells from the bottle's neck, using narrow ribbon. Top it off with a festive bow.

Mixed nut jar. Select a large jar, and paint the cover gold. Fill the jar with mixed nuts. Lightly brush assorted nutshells with gold paint. Cover the lid with gold holly, loops of ribbon, and the nuts, using hot glue.

Secure loops of wire to garlic cloves or pepper pods, using hot glue. Or pierce items with needle just below stem and insert wire through hole. Twist ends to form loop.

Secure wired items at various heights, tying narrow ribbon through the wire loops. Accent with jingle bells.

Secure cascading nuts to looped 24-gauge wire, using hot glue.

Create personalized labels with decorative papers, using rub-on transfer letters. Cut labels ½" (1.3 cm) larger than existing bottle labels, using scissors with decorative-edge blades. Cut small shapes, using paper punches. Spray adhesive on label; position as desired. Smooth out any air bubbles.

PLACEMAT TABLE RUNNER

This innovative table runner adapts simply to the various needs of your holiday season. Join four 18" (46 cm) sections, using elegant frog closures or buttons and bows, for a 72" (183 cm) table runner. Remove the center sections and use them as placemats for a quiet dinner for two; leave the end sections joined for a short runner. Or create additional rectangular sections, as desired, for a longer runner and more place settings.

Select fabrics according to the feeling you wish to convey; jacquards or tapestries provide elegance; metallics are striking; cotton prints may add a touch of the country. Choose frog closures or buttons and ribbons to complement your fabric. Frogs are available in a variety of colors and metallics. Button styles range from plain to fun holiday shapes to metals and fancy jewels.

Metallic print fabric in the placemat table runner at left is connected with glimmering frogs. Ribbon-tied buttons on the star-spangled runner (above) are easily disconnected to set the table for two.

HOW TO MAKE A PLACEMAT TABLE RUNNER

MATERIALS

* ⅞ yd. (0.8 m) fabric, for front.
* ⅞ yd. (0.8 m) lining fabric.
* Polyester batting.
* Six frogs, or twelve buttons and 3 yd. (2.75 m) of ¼" (6 mm) ribbon.
* Two tassels.

CUTTING DIRECTIONS

Cut four 19" × 14" (48.5 × 35.5 cm) rectangles from each fabric and batting.

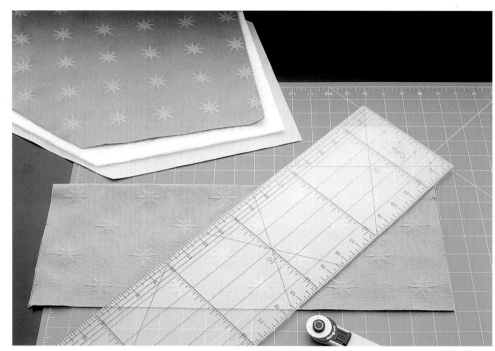

1 Fold one front rectangle in half lengthwise. Mark point 7" (18 cm) from corner on long cut side; align straightedge from end of fold to mark, as shown, and cut. Repeat with second front rectangle, two lining rectangles, and two batting rectangles, for two end sections.

2 Place one front end on one batting end, right side up. Position tassel at point so cord loop extends beyond cut edges; secure with pins. Place one lining end on front, right side down, aligning all raw edges; pin.

3 Stitch ½" (1.3 cm) seams around all sides, leaving 5" (12.5 cm) opening on short side; pivot each side of tassel cord, and stitch straight across point.

5 Repeat steps 2 to 4 for remaining end section and two rectangular sections; omit tassel on rectangular sections. Press; tuck seam allowances in at openings. Slipstitch openings closed. Topstitch ¼" (6 mm) from all edges.

4 Trim batting close to stitching; trim ½" (1.3 cm) batting at opening. Trim seam allowances at corners; press seam allowances open. Turn right side out.

6 Buttons and ribbon. Stitch two buttons on each short side, 2¾" (7 cm) from corners. Cut six 18" (46 cm) lengths of ribbon. Wrap ribbon in figure eight around two adjacent buttons; tie bow.

6 Frogs. Position two loops on short side of one end and both center sections, 2¾" (7 cm) from corners; position frog buttons on adjacent sections, as shown. Secure frogs with hand stitches.

CASCADING FRUITS & ROSES

Make an elegant statement with this cascading pedestal arrangement of roses, ivy leaves, and glittering fruits. Arrange the stems in a crystal stand so the fruits sweep through the ivy.

Purchase assorted fruits in clusters and on long stems; decorate them with a fine glitter, such as DecoArt™ Glamour Dust™. Cut individual blossoms from rose stems and place them at the top of the arrangement. Accent the arrangement with clusters of fragile, dried pepper berries, available in several colors.

HOW TO MAKE A FRUITS & ROSES ARRANGEMENT

MATERIALS

* Three different artificial fruit stems, such as lime, pear, and miniature orange.
* Grape clusters.
* Craft glue; flat paintbrush, about ⅜" (1 cm) wide.
* Fine glitter; sheet of paper.
* Floral Styrofoam®, 4" × 4" × 1½" (10 × 10 × 3.8 cm); serrated knife.

* Crystal compote or cake stand.
* Floral adhesive clay, floral stem wire, floral tape; wire cutter.
* Crystal marbles.
* One ivy plant with long stems.
* Pepper berries in desired color; hot glue gun, optional.
* Artificial rose stems with assorted blossoms.

1 Dilute craft glue slightly with water. Brush glue on fruit surface. Sprinkle fruit with fine glitter while glue is wet; shake excess glitter onto paper. Apply glue and glitter to all fruits; pour excess glitter back into bottle as necessary. Allow fruit to dry.

2 Trim Styrofoam block to sit level in compote, using serrated knife; trim height to level of compote rim. Secure foam to bowl of compote, using floral adhesive clay. Pour marbles around foam. Insert ivy into center of foam; arrange stems around compote as desired.

(Continued)

3 Break pepper berry stems about 1½" (3.8 cm) from berries. Wrap stem wires to berry stems, using floral tape; stretch tape slightly. Make several clusters. Glue broken clusters together, if necessary, using hot glue. Trim wire stems to various lengths, from 8" (20.5 cm) to 24" (61 cm) as desired.

4 Insert two fruit stems near side of foam top; insert third stem near other side. Insert one short berry stem on each side. Insert long berry stem on side with one fruit stem. Bend stems to follow curve of ivy stems; conceal stems, using ivy.

5 Cut stems of large and medium roses to 5" (12.5 cm); if stem is shorter than 5" (12.5 cm), extend stems as in step 3. Insert large rose at center, facing up; insert medium roses at center right, facing sides. Bend or trim taller stems so they fall below visual lines of dinner guests.

6 Cut two rosebud stems to 3" (7.5 cm), one to 6" (15 cm), and one or two to 15" (38 cm); extend stems as in step 3, if necessary. Insert short stems in front of medium roses; insert medium stem near large rose; insert long stems into sides.

7 Drape grape clusters over compote rim sides. Secure any rose leaves trimmed from floral stems to wire stems; insert as desired to fill gaps. Trim longest elements, if desired.

Secure moss-covered foam to top of decorative pedestal, about 5" × 14" (12.5 × 35.5 cm) tall. Trim longer stems, if desired; add additional fruit stem if you wish to view the arrangement from all sides. Weave decorative ribbon throughout stems.

Use a shallow bowl or ceramic urn, and place it at the end of the mantel. Gild leaves and fruits lightly, using wax-based paint. Drape stems part-way across the mantel while allowing others to cascade down the fireplace side. Substitute rose leaves for blossoms and berries at back; scatter gilded nutshells among leaves.

VARIATIONS FOR THE FRUITS & ROSES ARRANGEMENT

MITTEN GIFT BAGS

These small gift bags are so delightful when hung on Christmas tree branches, you may want to hang several pairs! Tuck special gifts inside or fill them with wrapped candies.

Select nonwoven fabrics that do not ravel, for fast and easy sewing without seam finishing. Choose from a variety of polar fleece, felt, or synthetic suede fabrics in solids, subtle sculpted textures, and multicolored prints. Cut single layers of fabric with scissors or a rotary cutter to avoid shifting layers.

Choose woven fabrics, if desired, and finish the mitten seams and upper edge to prevent raveling. Vary the look with embossed velvets, flannels, or corduroys.

Purchase a boa of marabou feathers, the very soft, fine down of storks, at fabric and costume supply stores. Or use a narrow strip of knit fur fabric for the mitten's trim.

HOW TO MAKE A MITTEN BAG

MATERIALS

* ¼ yd. (0.25 m) fabric.
* Scissors; rotary cutter and cutting surface, optional.
* ¼ yd. (0.25 m) marabou feathers or 2" × 9" (5 × 23 cm) fur fabric, for trim.
* ¼ yd. (0.25 m) satin ribbon, ⅛" to ¼" (3 to 6 mm) wide, for hanger.

1 Cut two mirror-image pieces for mitten palm and mitten back, using pattern on page 124. Place palm on back, right sides together, aligning raw edges; pin. Stitch, using ¼" (6 mm) seam allowances; pivot at each side of thumb, and leave upper edge open. Finish seam, using zigzag stitch, if desired. Clip seam allowance to pivot points above and below thumb. Turn mitten right side out.

2 Place marabou trim on outside of mitten with core about ⅜" (1 cm) from upper edge. Whipstitch core to mitten, starting at outer wrist seam; avoid trapping feathers beneath stitches. Cut excess trim. Or hand-stitch fur strip near mitten edge.

3 Fold 9" (23 cm) ribbon in half; secure ends to seam allowance of outer wrist. Wrap small items in tissue or iridescent cellophane, if desired; hang from tree branch.

PAINTED SANTA GIFT BOXES & BAGS

These merry gift boxes and bags repeat the three-dimensional design of the patchwork Santa tree skirt (page 48) and wall quilt (page 72). Set them under the tree or throughout the house, filled with holiday mementos or treats. Or gift a friend and share the merriment of the holiday season.

Choose from a variety of unpainted wood, papier mâché, or heavy paperboard square boxes. Or select a papier mâché gift bag, available in craft stores. Paint the simple design quickly. Add a precut wood oval nose to designs 4½" to 8" (11.5 to 20.5 cm) square, or cut smaller noses to desired size from thin balsa wood. Shape Santa's spectacles around a small sturdy cylinder such as a nail polish bottle. Replace plain bag handles with festive wired ribbon handles tied in a bow.

MATERIALS

- Unpainted container.
- Acrylic sealer.
- Graphite paper; straightedge; painter's masking tape, optional.
- One 1¼" (3.2 cm) wooden oval, or ¹⁄₁₆" (1.5 mm) balsa wood and mat knife; craft glue.
- Acrylic paints; green, red, white, black, as desired for face.

- Texturizing medium, optional.
- 12" (30.5 cm) 24-gauge brass wire, for glasses; firm cylinder.
- Acrylic spray sealer.
- One brass jingle bell.
- 2 yd. (1.85 m) gold wired ribbon, ½" (1.3 cm) wide, for gift bag.

HOW TO MAKE A SANTA FACE PATTERN

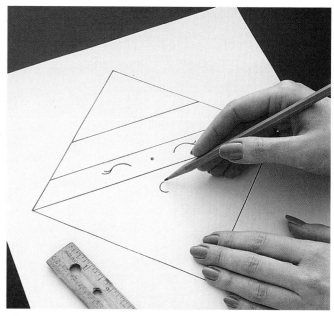

1 Trace box lid on paper. Draw diagonal line from corner to corner. Draw two lines parallel to first line, ⅞" and 2" (2.2 and 5 cm) above it. The small triangle at the top is the hat; below the hat is the trim, face, and beard. Adjust lines to suit box size.

2 Mark nose position at center of face. Draw two ¾" (2 cm) arcs, for eyes; start each ¾" (2 cm) from center. Add two short lines, as shown, for lashes. Draw ⅜" (1 cm) circle ½" (1.3 cm) from face, directly below nose position, for mouth.

HOW TO MAKE A SANTA BOX

1 Apply acrylic sealer to box; allow to dry. Make pattern as shown above. Transfer pattern to box lid, using graphite paper; extend lines onto sides of lid.

2 Cut small nose from balsa wood, using mat knife, if desired. Paint box bottom, hat, face, and nose; allow to dry. Apply painter's masking tape along edge of hat and face, if desired. Paint trim and beard. Apply texturizing medium, if desired. Remove tape; allow paint to dry. Paint mouth.

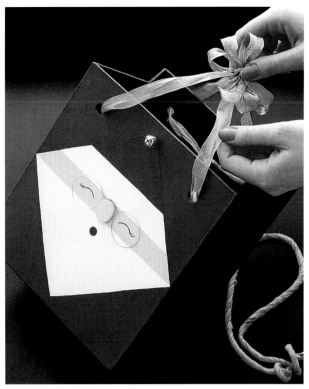

3 Make wire spectacles, following steps 6 to 8 on pages 52 and 53. Attach nose at center mark and secure spectacles over nose, using glue. Paint eyes; allow to dry overnight. Spray container with two coats acrylic sealer, following manufacturer's directions. Glue jingle bell to tip of hat.

For gift bag, remove bag handles, if any. Follow steps 1 to 3. Cut ribbon in half, and thread through bag's holes; tie in bow.

PATTERNS

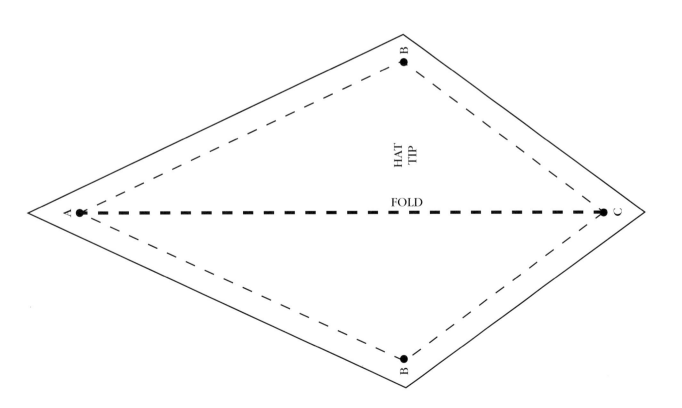

B

A

FOLD

C

HAT TIP

B

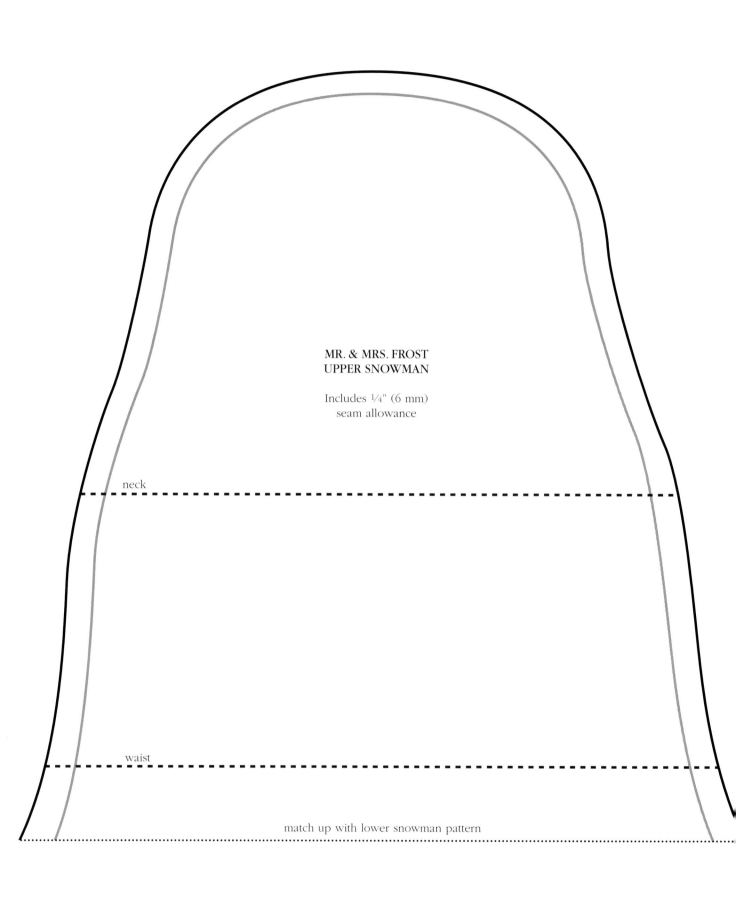

**MR. & MRS. FROST
UPPER SNOWMAN**

Includes ¼" (6 mm)
seam allowance

neck

waist

match up with lower snowman pattern

LOWER SNOWMAN

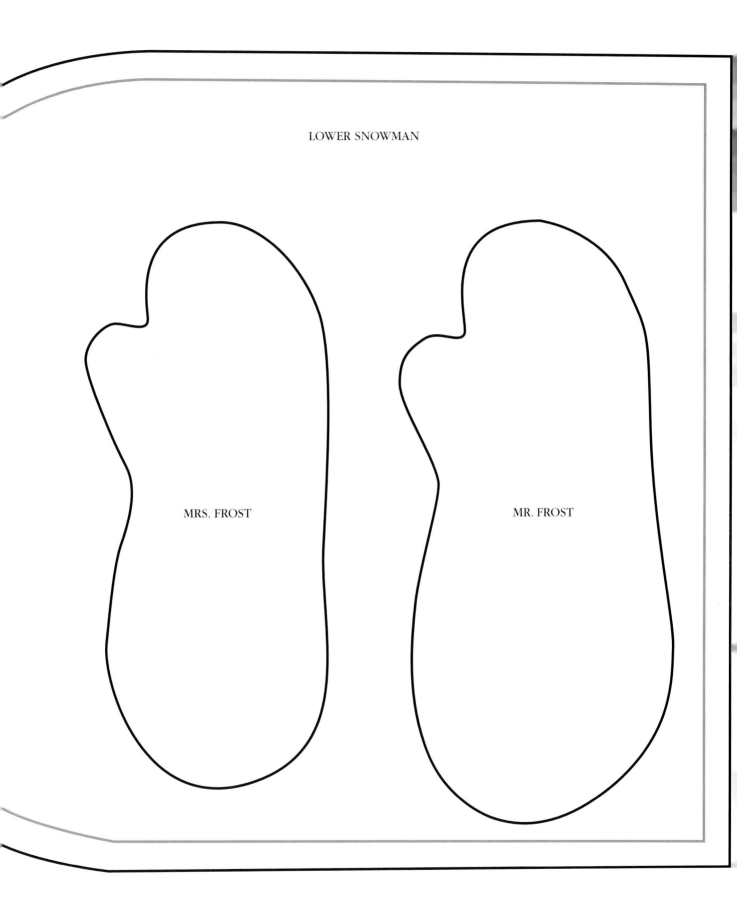

MRS. FROST

MR. FROST

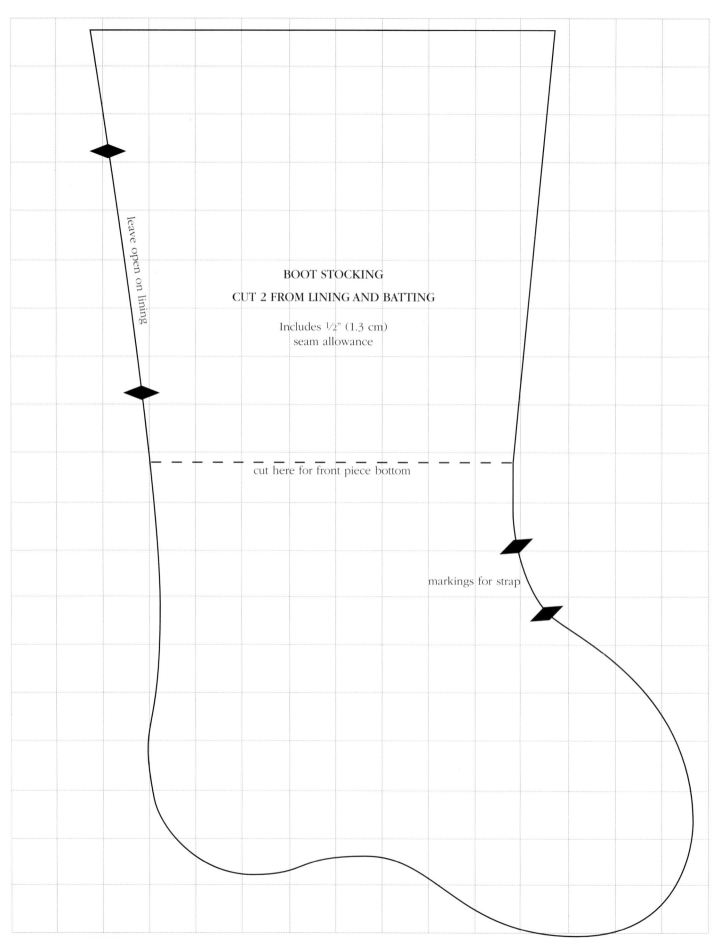

leave open on lining

BOOT STOCKING

CUT 2 FROM LINING AND BATTING

Includes ½" (1.3 cm)
seam allowance

cut here for front piece bottom

markings for strap

1 square equals 1" (2.5 cm)

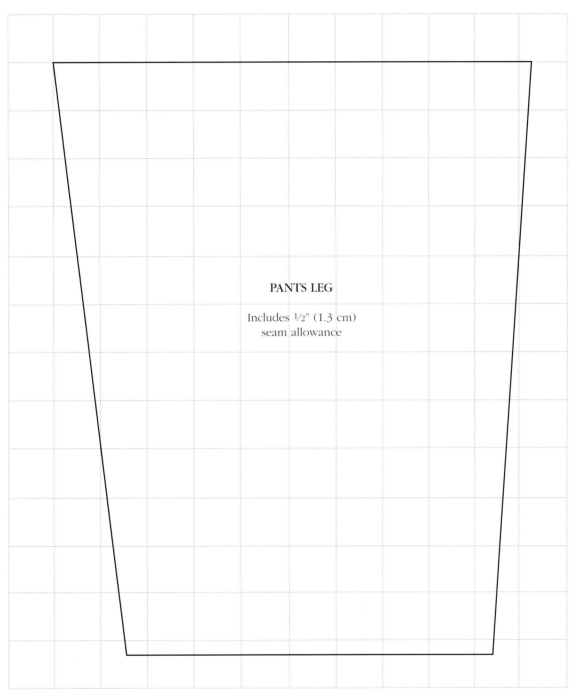

PANTS LEG

Includes ½" (1.3 cm)
seam allowance

1 square equals 1" (2.5 cm)

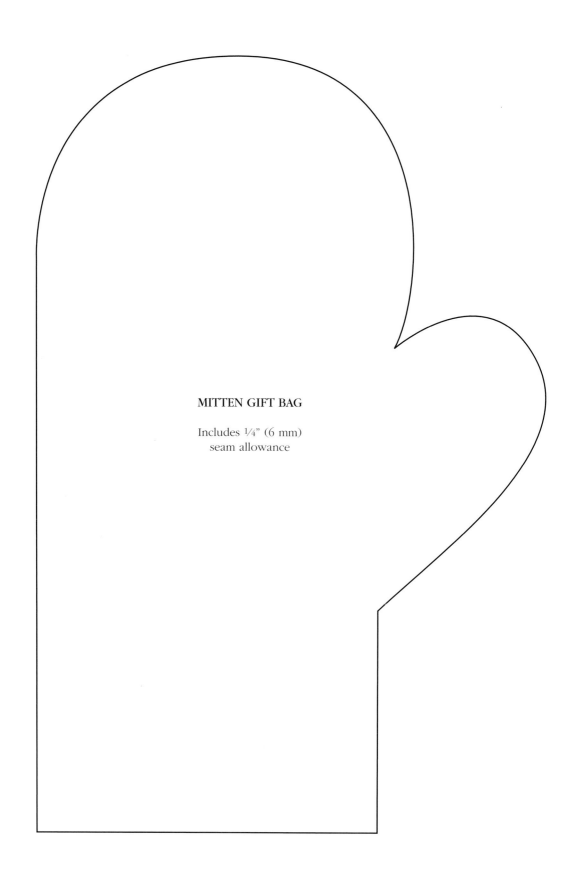

MITTEN GIFT BAG

Includes ¼" (6 mm)
seam allowance

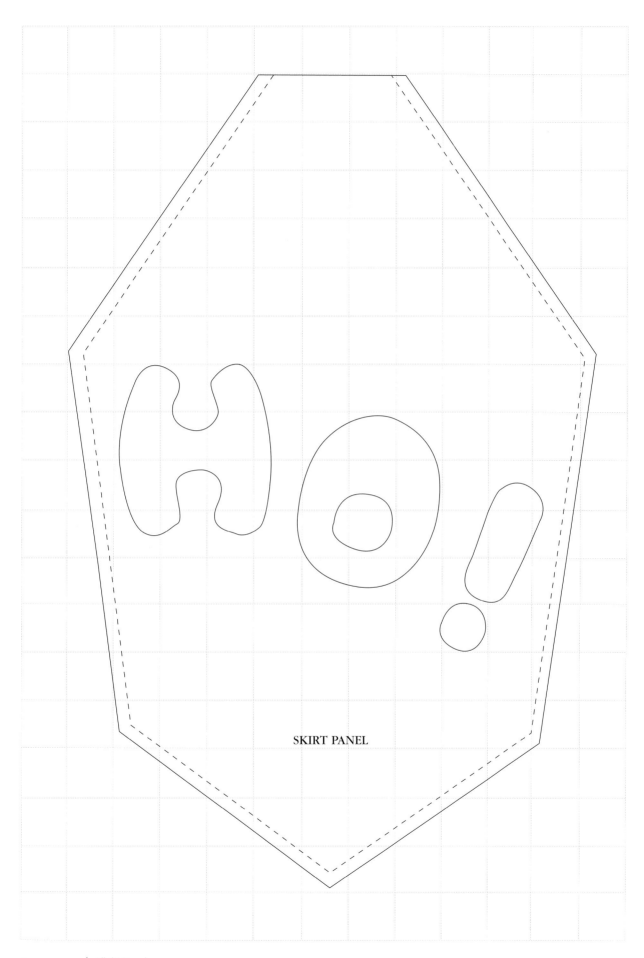

SKIRT PANEL

1 square equals 1" (2.5 cm)

INDEX

Vice President/Publisher: Linda Ball
Vice President/Retail Sales, Book Development: Kevin Haas
Executive Editor: Alison Brown Cerier

Project Manager: Amy Friebe
Senior Editor: Linda Neubauer
Senior Art Director: Stephanie Michaud
Writer: Nancy Sundeen
Copy Editor: Janice Cauley
Researchers: Dawn Anderson, Linda Grublesky, Teresa Henn, Christine Jahns, Carol Olson, Janice Rapacz, Ruth Reetz, Nancy Sundeen, Joanne Wawra
Lead Project & Prop Stylist: Coralie Sathre
Project & Prop Stylists: Bobbette Destiche, Christine Jahns, Joanne Wawra
Sample Production Manager: Elizabeth Reichow
Lead Artisan: Carol Pilot
Artisans: Margaret Andolshek, Diane Combites, Arlene Dohrman, Sharon Eklund, Jackie Kanuit, Virginia Mateen, Joan Wigginton
Senior Technical Photo Stylist: Bridget Haugh
Technical Photo Stylists: Kathleen Smith, Nancy Sundeen
Studio Services Manager: Marcia Chambers
Photo Services Coordinator: Carol Osterhus
Senior Photographer: Chuck Nields
Photographers: Paul Englund, John Lauenstein, Steve Smith
Photography Assistants: Jeffrey Krueger, Andrea Rugg, Kevin Timian
Scene Shop Carpenters: Troy Johnson, Greg Wallace, Daniel Widerski
Publishing Production Manager: Kim Gerber
Print Production Manager: Stasia Dorn
Mac Design Manager: Jon Simpson

Mac Designers: Laurie Kristensen, Amy Mules, Brad Webster
Production Staff: Curt Ellering, Laura Hokkanen, Kay Wethern
Contributors: Conso Products Company; Darice, Inc.; Offray Ribbon; Waverly, Division of F. Schumacher & Company

Printed by R. R. Donnelley
10 9 8 7 6 5 4 3

Library of Congress Cataloging-in-Publication Data
Tis the season.
      p. cm. -- (Arts & crafts for home decorating)
   Includes index.
    ISBN 0-86573-416-X (hardcover). -- ISBN 0-86573-417-8 (softcover)
    1. Christmas decorations. I. Creative Publishing International.
  II. Series.
  TT900.C4T57 1998   98-20187
  745.594' 12--dc21